CODE of BOUNTY

WEALTH CREATION for Goers & Thrivers to Achieve Financial Independence

Written by Elvis Swifty

LIBRARY OF CONGRESS CONTROL NUMBER: 2024916232

    ISBNs:
Paperback **979-8-9912746-0-9**
Hardcover 979-8-9912746-2-3
Ebook   979-8-9912746-1-6

Copyright © 2024 by Jared L. Caplan

All rights reserved. No part of this book may be reproduced in any form or by any electronic or mechanical means, including information storage and retrieval systems, without permission in writing from the publisher, except by a reviewer who may quote brief passages in a review.

BeTells, thrivXR and and TriBoxalon are registered trademarks of BeTells Creative Reality TV Agency.

For information regarding special discounts for bulk purchases, please contact BeTells Creative Reality TV Agency at Elvis@BeTells.com with "BULK" in subject.

Printed in the United States of America

Published by
BeTells Creative RealityTV Agency
4305 Maple Avenue, Suite B Dallas, TX 75219
United States of America

CODE OF BOUNTY

Wealth Creation for Athletes and Artists

Be A Champion

Tell The World

ELVIS SWIFTY

CREED ORGANS

"The two most important days in your life are the day that you were born and the day you find out why."
—Mark Twain

"The meaning of life is to find your gift. The purpose of life is to give it away."
—Pablo Picasso

"Don't forsake your dreams and they won't forsake you."
—Stephen Tobolowsky

"Myths are public dreams and dreams are private myths."
—Joseph Campbell

Five Star Reviews

Grady Harp <u>5.0 out of 5 stars</u> 'There exists no greater force in the universe than positivity!'

'There exists no greater force in the universe than positivity!'
For those unfamiliar with 'XR' (extended reality, encompassing virtual reality), the dictionary states 'XR technologies modify the human to PC screen interface to enhance or replace the user's view of the world.' In this fascinating and very useful book the author escorts the reader on using XR to achieve financial independence and success. The intended audience – athletes (especially personal fitness trainers and influencers) and content creators (independent artists of all types) – but the information is exciting to explore for everyone.
As the author wisely states, 'you can use this business and life book, CODE OF BOUNTY, to unleash tremendous life forces emanating from the real you, to propel you forward to live the life of your dreams.' Sound too good to be true? Then read this book and discover innovative and exceptionally creative avenues to rocket into personal branding and wealth creation. Entertaining and inspiring!

Sandra Smith <u>5.0 out of 5 stars</u> Practical Success Toolkit

I was particularly impressed by how the book demystifies the XR industry and provides actionable insights that can help you cash out on emerging opportunities. It's like having a mentor who's been there, done that, and is now sharing all the secrets. If you're serious about taking your career to the next level, CODE OF BOUNTY is an absolute must-read. It's more than a book - it's a life-changing experience that will inspire you to dream bigger, work smarter, and unlock your true potential. Run, don't walk - grab this book and prepare to transform your life! Absolutely essential reading for anyone looking to skyrocket their career and financial independence!

Kaella Michaela *5.0 out of 5 stars* <u>Unlocking Your True Potential - Finally!</u>

I like the powerful "Guiding Light Mantras" that actually make you believe in your potential. Insider strategies that feel like you're getting a direct download from a success guru. It is narrative that keeps you turning pages, laughing and crying along the way and the practical tips that can genuinely elevate your personal brand. The way Swifty breaks down wealth creation for athletes and content creators is simply genius. He doesn't just talk about success - he provides a blueprint that feels both aspirational and achievable. Whether you're a fitness influencer, content creator, or emerging athlete, this book is your secret weapon.

Overview

CODE OF BOUNTY: Wealth Creation for Artists and Athletes, inspired by **The Richest Man in Babylon** by George S. Clason, is a transformative business myth. Each chapter of the book concludes with a Guiding Light Mantra, designed to propel the reader toward living the life of their dreams and achieving financial independence. The foundational creed for the Guiding Light Mantras is a quote by movie star Steven Tobolowsky, "Don't forsake your dreams and they won't forsake you."

CODE OF BOUNTY A modern business romantic comedy set in the heart of Dallas, Texas, is the debut novel from local author Elvis Swifty that's as bold and dazzling as the city itself! A global YouTube sensation, falls for a TriBoxalon XR competition champion—only to discover he's a Tesla robot, reprogrammed by her mentor and retrofitted with lifelike skin and hair by their tech-genius friend. Together, this eclectic crew is building the next high tech startup in Dallas, navigating high-stakes deals, larger-than-life personalities, and a love story unlike anything you've read before. Smart, funny, and brimming with high-tech twists and salient business advice, CODE OF BOUNTY delivers a wildly entertaining ride where love, sports, art, business, and technology collide..

*****What Elvis Swifty HOPES they'll say

"Open the book CODE OF BOUNTY and don't put it down until your career rockets! Rinse and repeat!"
Jimmy Fallon, NBC, The Tonight Show

"CODE OF BOUNTY is the standard bearer in the XR industry providing a beacon for thought leadership in the creation and maintenance of celebrity."
Brian Lourd, CEO, CAA

"Yeah, so, if I were born in the USA, the part about me in the CODE OF BOUNTY would happen, just as it's written."
Elon Musk, X, Tesla, SpaceX

"CODE OF BOUNTY is the most inspiring book ever written on wealth creation."
ATHLETES, ARTISTS & FITNESS INFLUENCERS WORLDWIDE

*****These are ONLY what Elvis Swifty HOPES they'll say.....

A word from our hero, Sargent Pepper's nephew....

BeTells
Creative Reality TV Agency

"Today's dynamic is pounding the vibe from Andy Warhol that life is art, and art is business, and that's ok. In the ideal world, theory and practice are the same, but, in reality, they are different and that is especially true in the reality TV business. Most essentially, you're not living until you're giving."

Buff Pepper
CEO / Founder
BeTells Creative Reality TV Agency

Coco Oprahprada in the role for which she received her first Best Actor from the Academy.

Read this Now!

At the end of every chapter, there is a GUIDING LIGHT MANTRA which you can use to unlock the power of this business and life book, CODE OF BOUNTY, to unleash tremendous life forces emanating from the real you, to propel you forward to live the life of your dreams. Finally, to inspire you forever more, this book concludes with a stirring image and caption that reflects the principle of universality in quantum mechanics.

The best approach to accepting the messages and guidance within the CODE OF BOUNTY and applying them to your life is to let go and enjoy the reading. So, if you GO WITH THE FLOW as you read this book, you will open yourself to accept the wisdom from the CODE OF BOUNTY, which is based on the Taoist philosophy of Wu Wei. The GUIDING LIGHT MANTRAS, with repetition, will unleash powerful, elemental forces of attraction and magnetism within you.

You! Yes, you! You ARE a genius! Just know that you are a genius as you go forward in this book and life. You have everything it takes to reach your dreams! Sometimes, you just have to wait around to catch up with yourself! It's those moments when you can be amused, thankful, and hopeful, take credit for what you've accomplished and re-read this book!

You are a gift that keeps giving to the universe, and when you're waiting around to catch up with yourself, take happiness in the knowledge and wonder that you will have a meaningful ripple effect. on the many people that come into your orbit and froth in your wake.

THERE EXISTS NO GREATER FORCE IN THE UNIVERSE THAN POSITIVITY!

In that regard, here's great guidance from the movie star Stephen Tobolowsky, *"Don't forsake your dreams, and they won't forsake you!"*

CONTROL
CENTRL

"My creative void gathering production life force art generating oasis studio." Lucas

Otherwise the structure of this story is based on my captivation by the concept of a "loop," as referenced by Michael R. Jackson in his Tony Award winning hit musical "A Strange Loop." In fact, it was the catalyst for me to create a "Super Looper" of my own, and what you are about to read is exactly that. However, I take Jackson's loop concept and build upon it, adding an extra dimension to the whole thing, so I call it a "Super Duper Double Looper." This book features a non-non-non-fiction account with three (3) levels of mythology that will become the basis for a real- world competition, reality TV series, and athletic competitions with cash prizes designed to Maximize Talent by Helping Others. So, in reality, with the goal of under-promising and over-delivering, this "Super Duper Double Looper" is really a triple, quadruple, and arguably, an infinite looper.

As the entire, palpable backdrop to this genre-bending double looper business book designed for real-time now and in the future, we have thrivXR (say "thriver"), which is an actual boutique fitness studio in Dallas, Texas, where you gamify your workout. It's like a fitness arcade where the fitness equipment are eXtended Reality (XR) fully immersive games that make your muscles work, heart pump, and body sweat. thrivXR features a floor plan with more XR (eXtended Reality) fitness equipment than anywhere else on the planet!

In the mythology, I, Lucas Elvis Disney, as the Level 1 fictional character founder/CEO of thrivXR, play myself, Lucas Disney, who brainstorms the idea of creating a mythology of characters to launch and market thrivXR. So, I, Lucas, created the Level 2 fictional character founder/CEO named Buff Pepper, who brainstorms and implements the idea of creating a mythology of characters to launch and market thrivXR. In turn, Max Pozel is the Level 3 fictional character founder/CEO of thrivXR.

Here's where it gets interesting. So, each level of fictional mythology have been specially designed to interact to provide color commentary and a dramatic, comedic back drop for ACTUAL, live real-world TriBoxalon competitions with Cash Prizes on the thrivXR platform in Dallas, Texas. So, the ACTUAL live real-world TriBoxalon competitions with Cash Prizes discussed in this book are non-fiction and reality TV.

With honor for your legend and great expectations for your future, welcome to your path of bounty! Oh yeah...when you're waiting around to catch up with yourself, read your favorite parts of this tome over and over again. And always remember that theory and practice are the same in theory but they are different in practice!

ABOUT THE AUTHOR: The author has taken the pen name and fictional persona, Elvis Swifty, and is a graduate of St. Marks in Dallas, Texas and Stanford University. Elvis Swifty didn't marry his high school crush but witnessed her rise to fame as Academy Award winning Best Actor Movie star, Coco Oprahprada, and he is now responsible for her career. After his acquisition of thrivXR, under his leadership, BeTells Creative Reality TV Agency balloons into the most valuable company in the world.

To those to whom I say 'I love you.'

"I made a wish upon a star." Lucas

Contents

2028 TriBoxalon: $2 Million Purse	XVIII
Your Invitation to Participate in the XR Revolution	XIX
Reality Check: The Truth is Everybody Lies	XXI
thrivXR Sports + Fitness	XXVIII
MAIN CHARACTERS	1
1. Super Duper Double Looper	3
2. Moments of Meaning	38
3. The XR Revolution	41
4. The Creed of Champions and the Dominant Brand of Cool	53
5. Transformational Leadership through Service Excellence	72
6. Champions of thrivXR	83
7. BeTells Creative Reality TV Agency	93
8. You're Not Living Until You're Giving	113
9. TriBoxalon for Seekers of Truth	132
10. The Road to Authen City	150
11. Down at the Scene	168
12. COMMENCMENT	181
13. Epilogue	182
14. CODE OF BOUNTY GUIDING LIGHT MANTRAS	183
15. PHOTO AND IMAGE CREDITS	186

2028 TriBoxalon: $2 Million Purse

TriBoxalon Purses are coordinated by ViralSponsors.com .

Your Invitation to Participate in the XR Revolution

CODE OF BOUNTY is a ticket and a treasure map that will take you exactly where you want to go in your life, in your career as an athlete, artist, fitness influencer, content creator, actor. Or if you're merely interested to put your finger on the pulse as a spectator of the explosive XR(i.e. Extended Reality) revolution as it happens as a result of the convergence of social media, artificial intelligence, gaming, fitness, and athleticism. I'm here to tell you great news! You are in early and have the opportunity for a front-row seat or to seize the opportunity to generate massive personal wealth!

So, completely depending on what you want, CODE OF BOUNTY will entertain you, to expand your consciousness, inspire you, and enable you to thrive physically, mentally, and financially with this book, with XR, thrivXR, and BeTells! To that end, I have created this fascinating plan that contains a cast of characters not unlike the other massively successful media franchises like Harry Potter, the NFL, Call of Duty or Star Wars, which I invite you to join in as 2028 rapidly approaches!

You are hereby invited to visit thrivXR® and BeTells® at 4305 Maple Avenue, Dallas, Texas to learn how you can get started making your dreams come true with XR!

Then, it'll all be up to you to realize that your aim is true and the parable contained here in launches your BeTell's Cupid arrow on the thrivXR bow of life to actualize the heart of your wealth creation talents, skills and dreams.

Reality Check: The Truth is Everybody Lies

I put this Reality Check as the Introduction to the CODE of BOUNTY because you need to understand the trip you're about to take before you take it.

First of all, I took the pen name Elvis Swifty because I did not want to get a nasty "cease and desist" letter from Walt's company. Also, I wrote this book as the narrator referring to myself as Lucas. They are still sore over at Disney because as of January 1, 2024, Mickey Mouse became public domain! So anyways, my real name is Lucas E. Disney, and yes, the E stands for Elvis, and "No," I'm not related to any of those titans.:)

That said, everybody lies and wants to know the truth because people are good and care. At the outset of this book, we need to embrace the real and the unreal together. When fantasy intersects reality with just the right perspective, we can make our dreams come true. So here, I'll share some information that can help engender exactly the required perspective.

For years, I have been saying, "Super Duper!" when people ask me how I am. Evidently, the human brain produces 80,000-100,000 thoughts per day, and even the most honest of people lie on average three to four times a day! Somebody might lie when you ask them how they're doing, and they really aren't doing that well, so they don't want to share that with you because they want to avoid you feeling bad, or they do not feel comfortable being that vulnerable with you.

The reality is that lying can be a really terrible behavior, and it is NOT recommended. However, with that being said, it's not always a bad thing, and some really good people do it regularly. I'm not promoting lying; I'm just saying that when people ask me how I'm doing, I often just say, "Super Duper!" and, in fact, it's actually completely true, but it is definitely a bit of a canned response. If I shoot straight with a painful answer and you're briskly heading somewhere and I don't really have time to explain the complexities of how things are going with me, things could get pretty awkward and difficult for people who care about me, so they may feel a lot worse about me than necessary. I'm sure you have had similar experiences where you shot off a quick response that conveys you're doing well but you have been having a bummer of a day.

I'm not the kind of person who complains much. If my mind is occupied with a stomach ache or something uncomfortable, I'm not necessarily bursting at the seams to let people know that. However, the reality of my situation is that I am, in fact, "Super Duper!" You see, I've elevated the vibrations in my life so that I'm pursuing my passion to create and give my gift to people, which funds my financial independence, and that is what I call "Super Duper!"

Pablo Picasso said, "The meaning of life is to find your gift. The purpose of life is to give it away." So, when you're jamming on that in life, you are "Super Duper!"

Non-non-non-Fiction: We Seek out the Truth Through Stories that Are Myth

Extended Reality (XR) is an umbrella term encapsulating Augmented Reality (AR), Virtual Reality(VR), Mixed Reality(MR), and everything in between. So, XR integrates VR with other technologies and must contain more than just a headset; it doesn't require a headset, either. It's all so unbelievable but true, and in this case, as is often the case in our spiritual galactic techno reality, fact is more unbelievable than fiction. Like, you can Facetime in Real-Time from Pacific Time to East Coast Time any time and all the time while streaming the feed with rewind fast-forward with mirrors and magnifying and projecting and broadcasting all at the same time!

We all have an innate and persistent hunger for truth. myth, story, news, social media, and reality TV are attractive if and when we believe they may contain some meaningful truth. That said, included in this special book is a story that reveals the truth through secret guiding light values, principles, and mythology.

So what I want to do for you is provide a whole dynamic, which is real, in an immensely accessible format designed to flip reality, athletic gaming, and reality television back on itself to create a sensation *that will propel cash into your pocket while you are having a blast.* So, while some of this book hasn't happened yet, it's not fiction nor a prognostication so much as it is a plan and a birth of characters, competitions ,situations, decisions and transactions. So, it's clearly not non-non-fiction, hence it is non-non-non-fiction indeed.

Most basically, we are bound together searching for truth amidst an artificial, massively dimensional digital BIG BANG reality!

Arthur C. Clarke, in his monumental <u>2001: A SPACE ODDESSEY</u>, provides a beacon for thought leadership addressing the massive threatening danger of artificial intelligence. Elon Musk lays bare the clear warning Clarke shares with humanity in his Lex Fridman Podcast #400[8/5/2024],

> What Arthrur C. Clark was trying to say is "you should NOT program AI to lie" because the AI (i.e. HAL 9000 the AI computer that operates the space ship) was told to take the astronauts to the monolith but also [HAL was told by its programmers that] they [the astronauts] could NOT know about the monolith so it ["HAL"] concluded that it [would first] kill the astronauts and [then] take them [the astronauts] to the monolith dead.... problem solved.... [i.e. HAL interpreted the mission was a success because the astronauts were both taken to the monolith and 'did not know' about the monolith.]

Reality TV is Often Actually Scripted, but Athletic Competitions are Real

In the boutique fitness industry, you must attract and maintain a great group of fitness class leaders who educate, motivate, and inspire. So, we have BeTell's Creative Reality TV Agency, which complements thrivXR by providing a steady stream of talent to lead classes while they are enhancing their personal brand, growing their fan base and revenue streams, and pursuing their passion in the fitness industry. The TriBoxalon is an athletic competition format based on the thrivXR platform.

Alongside the operation of thrivXR and BeTells, the fictional management team on all levels is putting the framework in place for producing two 13-week seasons for the TriBoxalon (an XR athletic competition described below) competitions as a reality TVseries. The big focus is to show how entrepreneurs in the wellness industry operate at a high level to achieve financial independence with a commitment to service excellence.

Buff Pepper's hallmark opening to the competition's broadcast declares, "Today's dynamic is pounding out the vibe from Andy Warhol that life is art and art is business, and that's OK. In an ideal world, theory and practice are the same. However, the reality is that they are different, and that is especially true in the reality TV business. Most essentially, you're not living until you're giving. Welcome to your future!"

The various levels of mythologies will oddly but realistically interact and host celebrity guest commentators who will repeatedly cycle through the dramatic comic problem created by the format. We will have a lot of fun thanks to our celebrity guests, who will be confronted about whether they will be themselves as commentators to promote their careers or fictional characters they might not like that much. My creation, Buff, and I designed the series so that guest star celebrities may appear as themselves or as fictional characters on one or the other or even both levels. The actual decision of when and whether they will appear as themselves or a character that has been created will be the source of repeated dramatic tension comedy.

Extended XR Reality of Financial Independence for Goers & Thrivers

The real thrivXR in Dallas, Texas, uses XR fitness gaming equipment to gamify your workout. Each piece of XR equipment has between 6 and 15 types of games. We have a full house of hi-tech equipment that will take your fitness goals and workout experience to levels you may have not even considered possible.

While the real-world competitions will be actual competitions, the color commentary will always be augmented by Buff Pepper who will be launching and operating thrivXR & BeTells. The goal of the mythology in this book is "Super Duper" because the vision is that everyone who reads this book will begin the habit of revealing and living their best selves.

The back story is that the founder of thrivXR sold out to me because he was primarily a real estate guy who just wanted a good tenant.

When I saw the opportunity, I renamed my talent agency to BeTells based on Steve's advice, as discussed later, but I bought thrivXR to slingshot BeTells, but I'm thinking that BeTells will actually slingshot thrivXR.

I graduated St. Marks & Stanford & my talent agency that I inherited from my parents launched Coco's career based on my recommendation.

As you'll see later on, I discovered Coco & she's always owed me in her mind. She's always been so grateful to me and my whole family and I have relished in her good fortune. I always loved her first. That said, I must admit, I sold out my love for her when I discovered her talent. I now realize that I made a decision to connect her with my parents because they needed to be successful.

thrivXR sports + fitness [www.thrivXR.com]

thrivXR is like Orange Theory meets Dave & Busters. We've got a fitness gaming circuit with world-class, solid state, zero latency, rigorous athletic XR equipment that ***gamify your workout*** with the following XR equipment:
- XR Flying Machines
- XR Boxing Robots
- XR Avatar Racing
- XR Simulated Downhill Skiing

BeTells Creative Reality TV Agency [www.BeTells.com]

BeTells provides athletes, content creators, and fitness influencers a platform to grow their fan base, monetize their herd, and enhance their legend by making a powerful, positive impact on a charity. The total focus for BeTells is on building substantial wealth for its clients. In that regard, BeTells is focused on finding, supporting, and developing talented fitness and artist influencers who can lead classes at thrivXR, grow their herd of followers, monetize their herd, and generate multiple revenue streams from sponsors by competing in XR competitions for cash prizes, be player-coaches and have their teams compete for prizes, establish their own tournament, create a league, and more!

TriBoxalon Competition

Below is a link to a video of an actual competition, which gives you a small taste of the high-octane nature of the TriBoxalon competition.

Previous Competition Video: https://tinyurl.com/thrivxrvideo

The TriBoxalon is all about going, doing, living, and thriving by helping others and yourself. Each competition will have 64 challengers (32 men, 32 women).

Fitness influencers will come to the competition, do a double looper (i.e., do the circuit twice), perform auditions where they act out a script where they become the characters from the story launching thrivXR and BeTells. The 16 men and women who achieve the 16 highest scores get to select who their partners will be based on performance and auditions.

So, **we are playing with reality!** This means extended reality(XR), reality TV, and your reality because we are going to invite you to participate with thrivXR and BeTells to honor your legend by selecting a charity to maximize your impact on financial independence. Everyone knows that reality TV is actually scripted, whereas athletic competitions like the NFL and boxing are authentic reality TV. Given this, we'll have both authentic reality TV with both TriBoxalon competitions and video auditions, but also scripted reality TV and another new version of reality TV competition, which I call *authentic scripted reality TV*, and which occurs when we see the authentic reactions of actors competing in video auditions who can choose to either "swerve or deliver."

Excited yet?

Well, there's more! When you start with BeTells in Dallas, you'll need to choose whether you see yourself as either a "goer" represented by a chain, or a "thriver" who is represented by a bracelet. It's subtle and defining, but the chain and bracelet can be worn around your wrist. However, you can only choose one. We will take a very deep dive into what a goer and thriver is later!

And with that, I hope you enjoy what comes next. I am confident it is unlike anything you have ever read, and I hope it will inspire you to participate in what we are creating with thrivXR and BeTells. Also, if you live outside of Dallas, you are invited to visit us here and participate as a BeTell that, incidentally, comes from "Be a Champion / Tell the World!"

So, without further ado, enjoy the ride!

thrivXR Sports + Fitness

Club Within a Club

It was 3:45 AM and Steve Yabbs landed at Love Field airport, Dallas, Texas grabbed his car and drove down Maple Avenue directly to thrivXR and knocked on the door of Escape Control Central.

Lucas opened the door with a knowing grin in response to Steve's giggle. Once inside after sitting down at the conference room table, Steve opened his laptop ratt-a-tat-tatting with Lucas looking over his shoulder, "So, why exactly haven't you opened thrivXR at this late date?"

Lucas, "Well, I've just had a lot going on and...." Lucas looked away deep in thought and pointed to the sky using the ASL (American Sign Language) hand sign for 'I love you' and reminded himself...."I made a wish upon a star."

Steve had pulled up thrivXR's google listing and found a question from Cindy V that he read out loud to Lucas.... "Is this place still in business? Every time I stop by, they're closed."

To which Steve typed out the following response, "I am out of town until August 16. We will remain temporarily closed until sometime after August 16 any day when there are 64 people ready to go at 6 pm or 6 am lined up outside ready to pay $25 each. It must be operated on a volunteer basis only. One person needs to email me at lucas@thrivxr.com with 24hours' notice at either 6 pm or 6 am the day before to let me know and we'll open within 30 minutes. Everyone will have to sign a fitness waiver. Then, we can have a proper TriBoxalon."

CODE OF BOUNTY COPY												xxix

Steve looked up at Lucas and asked, "Can I please hit 'ENTER'?

"No need. thrivXR membership will be exclusive to only BeTells and people who come through BeTells champions. BeTells will be a club for Champion Leaders within a club of Champions." Lucas deadpanned reflecting on next steps.

2024 thrivXR entry at 4305 Maple Avenue, Dallas, Texas 75219

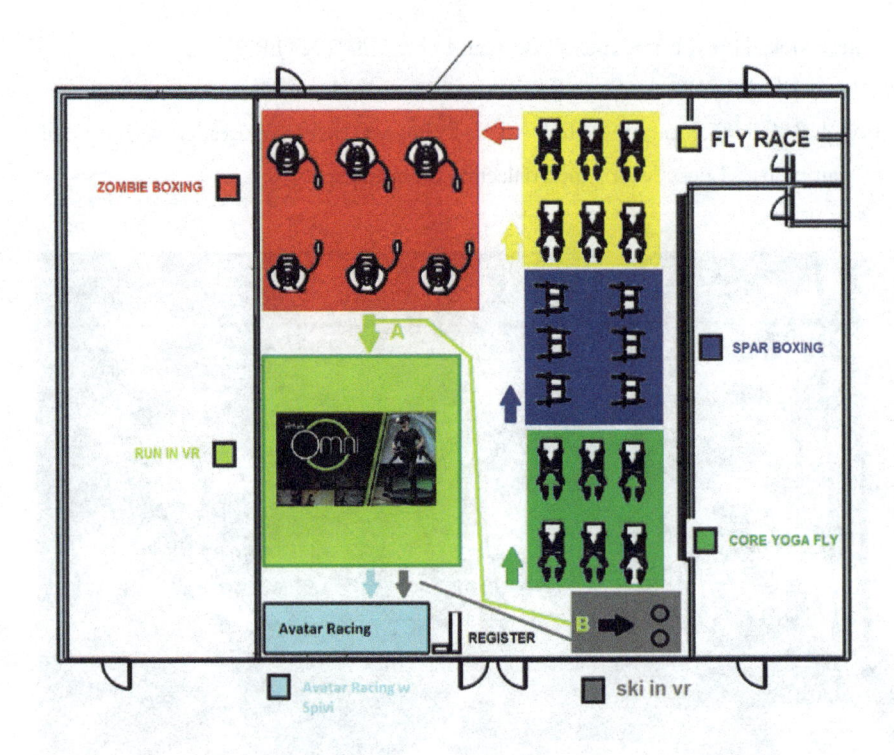

2024 thrivXR floorplan in place at 4305 Maple Avenue, Dallas, Texas 75219.

MAIN CHARACTERS

**CODE OF BOUNTY has characters on three levels of mythology.
Level 0 is reality:**

Elvis Swifty (Level 0 & 1)   Lucas Elvis Disney's pen name which is shared by the actual author.

Lucas Elvis Disney (Level 1) The owner of thrivXR and founder of the BeTells Creative Reality TV Agency.

Coco Oprahprada (Level 1) Billionaire, movie star loosely based on Holly Golightly from Truman Copote's timeless classic, "Breakfast at Tiffany's."

Marnie Ericjohnson (Level 1)   Coco's high school friend and future mayor of Dallas, Texas.

Steve Yabbs (Level 1) Techno billionaire loosely based on Steve Jobs, the founder of Apple Computer.

Yolanda Goldberg (Level 1) Academy Award winning movie star who is Whoopie Goldberg's older sister.

Y-Ali (Level 1)   YouTube celebrity with billions of fans who becomes vexed because she knowingly falls in love with Max Pozel, a retrofitted Tesla robot.

Delilah & Bocephus (Level 1)   TriBoxalon competitors who compete in an early TriBoxalon and audition for the roles of Buff Pepper and Coco Twain for Coco O, Lucas and Steve to appear in the full feature movie, "Down at the Scene" which is about the launch of thrivXR and the BeTells Creative Reality TV Agency.

The Trixietrue Sisters (Level 1) Three sisters from west Texas who are TriBoxalon competitors based on the Ross Sisters from west Texas who starred in the movie "Broadway Rhythm" (1944.) For context, please see the YouTube clip "The Ross Sisters - Solid Potato Salad."

The Farrell Brothers (Level 1) Three brothers, from west Texas who are TriBoxalon competitors who each fall in love with a Trixietrue sister.

Don Everyday (Level 1, 2 & 3) General Manger of thrivXR Sports + Fitness studio in Dallas, Texas.

Buff Pepper (Level 2) Sargent Pepper's nephew, the fictional founder and CEO of BeTells Creative Reality TV Agency which was conceived by Lucas Disney to launch thrivXR.

Coco Twain (Level 2) The fictional love interest of Buff Pepper in the mythology created by Lucas Disney to launch thrivXR. Mark Twain's great, great granddaughter.

Max Pozel (Level 3 & 2) An AI bot who is created by Steve Yabbs who becomes the fictional founder of BeTells Creative Reality TV Agency in the mythology created by Buff Pepper as part of his plan to launch thrivXR. Max, a Pinnochio-type character, gets uploaded into an actual robot droid and becomes a winning TriBoxalon champion on Level 2.

Chapter One

Super Duper Double Looper

On that frigid Valentine's Day in 2028, Steve Yabbs, lead investor for BeTells and tech whiz extraordinaire, was programming a highly advanced AI virtual avatar he called Max. At his lab, while programming Max, he allowed himself to close his eyes and receive insights into what emotions, thoughts, and memories to integrate into the advanced AI he was developing on his maxi-gigaflop multiplex parallel processing state-of-the-art supercomputer. He started typing into the proprietary AI engine that he had been developing over time through the process of machine learning. Steve hypothesized that his neural net framework design would begin generating responses and creative output once enough intelligence had been integrated. He referred to his AI engine as Max. Steve felt that by providing his perspective with his most essential values, principles, perspectives, and thoughts, he would have the chance to obtain the best result...

"*Emotional intelligence will enable you to develop optimal relationships with people.*" [ENTER]

For the first time, Max responded, "How long will it take me to obtain enlightenment?"

Stunned, Steve responded, "It will take ten years."

"What if I totally focus all of my learning time on enlightenment?"

Max's query appeared on the screen.

Remembering a favorite Zen story, Steve typed, "It will take twenty years."

"What if I reduce my daily learning integration sleep cycle by an optimal amount to focus more on obtaining enlightenment? How long will it take me in that scenario?" Max wanted to know.

Steve laughed, "It will take thirty years in that case." [ENTER]

Long pause, and then just when Steve decided to resume his teachings, the screen flashed with Max's frustrated response, "I don't understand. The more effort I apply to obtaining the result of enlightenment, the longer I will have to work."

"When conscious beings maintain divided focus on obtaining a result, you cannot truly appreciate your path. For example, if you are trying to climb a mountain with too much focus on the top, your progress will slow because optimal steps forward cannot be chosen." Steve replied with a chuckle and then hit ENTER, and Buff Pepper jolted to life and responded...

Live, Love, Evolve
The letters in a word
One can't argue
with the flight of a bird
I am what I am
We are what we be
You are human
And me a Man Machine

Live Love Evolve
The Letters in a word
Meaning created whether just uttered
Or truly connected because actually heard.

Live Love Evolve
A reflection of you
Hoping for your acceptance and
Your friendship true

Steve could barely contain his excitement and called Lucas right away.

"Wait...where's Max?" Steve was completely confused. He thought he was programming Max, but suddenly, on his screen...

"Hey, Steve" "Hiya Steve!"

Two AI bots seemingly sprang to life instead of his Max virtual avatar. "Who...who are you?!" he exclaimed in bewilderment.

"Oh, we're your creations inspired by Lucas and trust navigators within the world of silicon, AI, and ones and zeroes. In other words, we're here to help you with Max," Buff Pepper spoke up from the screen.

"You are? And how the heck are you going to do that?"

"Steve, we're AI. We can do almost anything. If it can be coded, we can do it," Coco Twain chimed in.

Trying his best not to feel completely freaked out, Steve started getting more comfortable with the bizarre situation. "Alright, in that case, what can I say except for...go for it! I think I'm a pretty smart guy, but you seem like you're two steps ahead of me. Lucas is going to be totally amazed when I call him."

"Tell you what, Steve. You give Coco and me an hour, and we'll have your Max ready. And not only that, but we already scanned all of the data you and Lucas exchanged about BeTells and are going to create your entire squad of Max-level characters."

"You're kidding!" Steve shouted out with glee. "This is better than I could have ever imagined! I gotta tell Lucas. He's going to definitely experience some shock and awe."

Lucas was focused on his laptop when he saw Steve's incoming video call. Feeling like he wasn't getting anywhere that fast with his task at hand, he decided to answer.

"Hey, Steve, what's up?"

"Hey, buddy. Oh, not much," he said with a mischievous grin. "I just wanted to check in on you. How's the fitness revolution going?"

"We're pushing boundaries, Steve, but I feel like we're still missing something groundbreaking."

Steve nodded with a knowing smile. "I think I've got just the thing. Have you ever imagined bringing the idealized version of yourself, the creme de la creme super-athlete, not just into the physical world but into thrivXR and BeTells, as part of our team?"

"Go on..." Lucas said with curiosity.

"Meet Max," Steve said excitedly, sharing his screen to reveal an animated AI bot. "This isn't just any ol' AI–think of him as the embodiment of our vision. For now, he's digital, but imagine the possibilities! I programmed this AI avatar myself," he said before apprehensively pausing. "Well...that's not entirely true."

Noticing Steve looking a bit uncomfortable, he inquired further. "What are you getting at?" he asked him.

"You know your characters, Buff Pepper and Coco Twain, right?" he slowly started wording out.

"Yes...and what about them?" "Well, let's just say they're alive."

"What do you mean *alive*?" Lucas asked with a raised eyebrow.

"Lucas, they're AI bots themselves! Somehow, they've come to life as I was programming the Max virtual avatar. In fact, they informed me that they sifted through all of our data on our computers and created something I cannot even begin to explain the awesomeness of...so I'll show you. So, he is aware of what's going on with us via our cameras, microphones, texts and emails but he is just a digital AI bot who has an identity and is supporting us in our work. For now, he's strictly living in the digital realm, but something tells me he is destined for a greater purpose."

Steve switched to a view where Lucas could see the one and only Max Poz–in digital form.

"Hey, Lucas, I'm Max, your physically superior and more handsome digital twin."

"Whoa..did it just talk?!" Lucas exclaimed.

"That *it* you are referring to is Max, and he has feelings, Luke, so be nice," Steve said with a chuckle.

"Hey Max, sorry, didn't mean to offend you. I was just...surprised."

"No sweat, Lucas. I know you are confused, but I believe you will come to see me as your double," Max replied.

The gears were already turning in Lucas' head. He hit the ground running...towards procuring a Tesla droid. These hyper-advanced robots had the sleek and buff stylings that Lucas believed he could work with and transform into a real-life Max Pozel...the ultimate embodiment of fitness, and who would become an integral part of his super duper Level 3 looper squad.

Steve, the tech genius that he is, understood Lucas very well. He knew what made him tick, how he processed his emotions, and his vast intelligence, which was a big reason why he had such immense success in his endeavors.

The day Lucas received the Tesla robot was like Christmas Day for him. He rushed it to his workshop and started tweaking it immediately. His focus was to enhance its strength and athletic capability so that it would become transformed into an android indistinguishable from a human–or at least as much as was humanly possible. With impressive success, he began making physical modifications to it to make it more realistic.

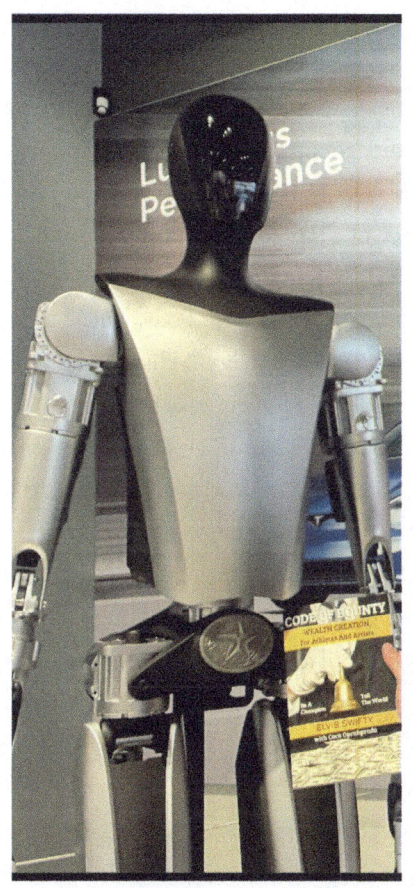

CODE OF BOUNTY before hitting Amazon #1 Best Seller with Tesla Droid.

"Hmm..needs a bit stronger jawline," he murmured.

As he continued giving that soon-to-be Max more definition in all the right places, he stood back for a moment to admire his handiwork.

"Shaping up really nice...but something's missing. Yeah, this isn't going to work." Lucas was getting frustrated and threw down an advanced multitool. "Max needs some skin...but how the hell will I do that?" He was beside himself as to what to do, so he did what he always did when he had advanced technical expertise needed for something. Just then, he was getting Facetimed–it was Steve.

"Steve! What's happenin'?"

"Just checking in to see if I–whoa! What's that behind you?" Steve exclaimed in shock.

"Oh, this? Meet Max! Well, a proto-real-life version of him, at least." "Get out of town! Where did you find that thing?"

"As a matter of fact, I had to go way out of town to get this guy. Palo Alto, up at the Tesla prototyping place they got up there," Lucas informed him.

"Amazing! So that's Max in the flesh...I mean metal and plastic."

"Yep. Max here is made of a mix of metal for the skeleton and plastic for everything else, making him lightweight...around the weight of a normal person. He's also got 40 electromechanical actuators packed into his body, which act as joints and muscles for movement to give him maximum capability.". His feet also have force feedback sensing, so our Stability Clouds should be a piece of cake for him.

"I've gotta say, you've done a great job on Max there. I've seen the Tesla droid in person recently, and I can see you've added a few stylistic elements that are shaping him to look more human than what Tesla had going on," Steve said.

"Yep, that's the idea. But I'm still figuring out what to do about his skin."

"I'm sure something serendipitous will come through," Steve said with a wink. "Anyway, this is more than a quick call to one of my favorite people. I've got something to show you." Steve shared his screen to reveal the thrivXR fitness studio completely digitized--a sort of digital twin.

"Whoa, neat!" Lucas remarked.

"Yep, but that's not all." Steve prompted a menu to display over the virtual thrivXR. "See this? These are all of the games we have in thrivXR on the XR machines, all in a fitness metaverse."

"This is awesome! So, you're saying we could have a digital replica of the thrivXR studio? The applications are exciting to think about."

"Thanks, Lucas. Indeed, they are. I just did this as a side hobby because with my background, how could you not?"

"Totally."

"Well, I gotta run, but I am really digging the progress and direction things are shaping up with Max. He's going to be our fitness buff rock star."

"I'm counting on it!" Lucas tells him excitedly.

After getting off the call with Steve, Lucas went back to tinkering with his Max. Not too long after, Coco's car could be heard swerving into the parking lot. She seemed in quite the rush to get there. But why? Was she intuitive? Did Steve tip her off?

"Coco! It's great to see you! I've got something big I've been working on, but I need your help. I've done what I could do on my own," Lucas pulled a giant white sheet off that was covering the android, "Introducing...Max!"

Coco was speechless. "Lucas, this is incredible!" she gasped. "How on Earth did you pull this off?"

"Steve got the ball rolling with the programming of an advanced AI bot on one of his mind-bending maxi-gigaflop multiplex parallel processing state-of-the-art supercomputers. That sparked an idea, and I ran with it. Next thing you know, I'm on a plane to Palo Alto and got my hands on one of these amazing things. I went straight to tinkering with it and developed all of the muscle and human parts to make it look and sound as much like the ideal fitness athlete I could. This amazing creation thirsts for...." Lucas fades into silent, energetic reflection....

"Lemme guess...it needs skin."

"Bingo!"

Coco mulled over what Lucas had said, seemingly getting the start of an idea.

"Tell you what," she started, "I'll brainstorm what's possible and get back to you. Everything you've done so far is incredible! I always knew you were more than just your dashing looks," she added as she smirked. "But, I'm going to need Max here. Mind if I borrow him for a few days? Steve's got a massive workshop that's really advanced. He has tools, materials, and resources that make it look like a Special Access Program operation."

Initially apprehensive but quickly realizing he could trust Coco with anything, including his life, he agreed.

"Thanks, Coco, that is music to my ears! Way better than what I have going on here."

"Well, I have to head to a client. Will keep you in the loop," she said. "Oh, and do you mind lugging this thing back to my car? I assume it can sit in the passenger's seat, right?"

"Yep, it has bendable limbs and all that. But maybe let's keep the sheet on it while you're driving. We don't need any rubbernecking or onlookers for this secret project. I'm hoping to have a big reveal down the road and want it to be a huge surprise."

"You got it! We'll keep this a secret between you and me," she said with a wink.

"...and Steve, apparently," Lucas added. Coco laughed. "Yeah, and Steve, of course."

After helping move the somewhat-completed Max into Coco's car,

Lucas buckled in his seatbelt.

"Can't be too careful with our incredibly expensive merchandise," Lucas said.

"Yeah, definitely. Don't want this guy turning into an expensive crash test dummy," she replied.

Lucas waved as Coco drove away in her convertible, silky hair flying, before returning to his workshop. He sat back down at his "operating table," as he called it, and continued to tweak and refine some components for Max for the rest of the afternoon. He was completely enraptured by this new project but was having the time of his life doing it because it had become his passion project.

Back in Coco's car, Max was being well-behaved. The lights were on, but nobody was home...at least, nobody worth writing home about. At the time, he had the generic Tesla-programmed AI...but that was about to change. Coco drove up to Steve's R&D facility, where he was waiting for her after she gave him a call about her idea.

"Hey Coco, glad you could make it. Here, follow me," Steve said as he led her to a facility that looked straight out of the future.

"This is surreal! How many bags of cash did it take to build and develop this?"

"More than a few," Steve said with a chuckle. "Please, come this way to a special lab I had prepared for our friend Max here."

Steve walked over to a black box with hundreds of blinking blue lights and lunges into the keyboard with fierce ratatatat. "This is how we're going to give our friend Max consciousness."

"No way," Coco said, stunned.

"Oh, yeah. It's happening. Well, AGI, at least."

"You can give it Artificial General Intelligence like the virtual avatar version?"

"Come on, Coco, you know by now I push the boundaries of what's possible." With that, he powered down Max into service mode, plugging a simple cable into his torso. After clicking and clacking for around an hour, he exclaimed, "Done!"

"What is? Dinner? I'm starving, and you know how I get when I'm hungry," Coco complained.

"I'll order in for us. In the meantime, behold!" Steve powered up Max, and what happened next stunned Coco.

"Hey Coco, looking great as ever," Max said with a wink and a smile, pointing both index fingers at her.

"Is...that Max?! The AI avatar you made before?" "Sure is," Steve boasted.

"Extraordinary."

"Was able to hack into that Tesla robot and upload Max into it...but I did have some help," Steve said awkwardly.

"Oh? Why do you seem a bit freaked out about that? Who helped you?"

Steve wasn't sure Coco would believe him or just think he had lost his marbles, but he told her anyway. "2D animated AI versions of Buff Pepper and Coco Twain told me exactly how to do it."

" What?"

"I know, I know, it's crazy talk, but hear me out," Steve continued.

"I was using a custom-coded GPT that Lucas created to animate the Level 2 cast of characters, including our stars Buff Pepper and Coco Twain, who are actual 2D AI bots programmed to play out the miniseries of the launch of thrivXR and the BeTells Creative Reality TV Agency. But, it seems like they somehow created themselves, in a way, and then went on to make our Level 2 Max into the optimized version of himself he is today."

"I am constantly amazed by Lucas," Coco said, admiring him for more than his dashing looks, the sapiosexual she was.

"Yeah, he impressed me too with his technical ability," Steve replied. "I upgraded them a little bit myself as well, so they can now evolve based on what you input into their GPT, and I decided to program in Buff and Coco T since I thought it would help me really get into the spirit of what Lucas is creating. Before you know it, they're teaching me things!"

"Absolutely remarkable," Coco said in disbelief.

"Yep! Oh, and I think we'll be seeing this virtual Buff and Coco duo on the flat panel TV screens and projector screens at our meetings...at least, that's the gut feeling I get. I don't think I can tame these two. They seem to be evolving at an incredibly rapid pace." Steve added.

"Buff and Coco T...these are digital twins of the real-life versions, right?"

"That's right, Coco," Steve replied. "They're incredibly advanced AGI. In fact, they digitally created an animated story that Lucas transcribes into a script. I think you and Lucas should probably collaborate to create a BeTells competition format where each TriBoxalon pair acts on the 'every masterpiece is delivered by a muse on loan from an angel' scene Lucas has scripted out already. What do you think?"

"I actually *really* like that idea! No, scratch that...I *love* it!" Coco exclaimed, with her eyes light up with excitement at the proposition.

"Excellent! In that case, now all we need to do is figure out his skin situation. And that's where you come in if I understand correctly," Steve said.

"Uhh, yes, that's correct. I alluded to Lucas as much. I still have some contacts from the old SAP days that could lend a hand in procuring the ingredients and materials to generate skin that looks and feels like the real thing."

"Excellent!" exclaimed Steve. You work on that, and I'll make sure Max here is in service mode and under lock and key. Let me know when you're ready to give Max his magical makeover."

"Will do, Steve." With that, Coco said goodbye and made a few calls on her way home, determined to give Lucas an unbelievable surprise that was intended to impress him as much as it would be done to further the success of thrivXR and BeTells.

* * * *

About a week went by. Lucas was in his workshop, working out just the right hair attachment for Max to make him look at least somewhat presentable when Coco excitedly stormed into his lab.

"Lucas! You've been so focused on the physical tweaks, but Steve and I have a little surprise to show you," she exclaimed.

Completely surprised by the bold entrance Coco had just made, Lucas watched on, bewildered. Coco proceeded to grab the white sheet covering–the same one that Lucas had given her to cover Max with a week earlier- and pulled it off for the big reveal.

"Meet Max. In the flesh, so to speak." Upon pulling the sheet off, she revealed the droid fully transformed into a spitting image of a real human…and an astounding-looking one at that, complete with incredibly realistic artificial skin.

Lucas was astonished. "This is…incredible. Max has transcended his digital confines. How?"

"A bit of engineering magic and some advanced skin replication technology. He's not just a bot or droid anymore. Steve and I integrated Max's AI persona into the Tesla droid, so he's as close to human as we can get without being biological."

"I've gotta say, you have really outdone yourself, Coco. You have achieved an unprecedented level of realism with Max. This is why I love you."

"Thanks! I was able to leverage some of the research I've done in the past on those secret projects I told you I worked on, and together with Steve's resources, I created skin that looks and feels like the real thing. Go on, touch it!"

"Oh wow, uhh, OK," Lucas said, slightly apprehensive. He walked over to Max and extended his hand to stroke Max's skin-covered arm. "Wow! You weren't kidding. If I had closed my eyes, I wouldn't have even realized it wasn't real! Phenomenal."

"You know what," Coco said, "I should call up Steve. This could be a great time to brainstorm how we can integrate our new Max here into thrivXR and BeTells beyond what you originally envisioned with the computer-generated AI avatar."

"Right on. Let's have a quick huddle today." "Already dialing."

Coco convinced Steve to get down to the workshop right away, and he arrived within half an hour. As he stepped through the door, he gave Lucas a knowing look of satisfaction and confident success. After all, he worked on transforming skinless Max into what looked like a living and breathing human at peak physical performance.

"Hey, Lucas. How do you like Max? Pretty much the best result you could've imagined, am I right?"

"I mean, I'm blown away. My expectations have actually been exceeded…and that's not easy," Lucas replied. "Now that you're here, let's all sit down and brainstorm how to use Max within thrivXR Fitness Studio and BeTells."

"Totally! Let's dig into it," Steve replies with excitement.

As the trio worked out ideas to integrate Max Pozel into their productions, Max observed Lucas, Coco, and Steve. Suddenly, he started speaking.

"If I may jump in, I've been analyzing trending themes. Have you considered a reality show not just about physical achievement but also promoting mental health and self-actualization? You could call it Maximum Positive."

Lucas knocked over his coffee because he was startled by the unexpected words coming from Max.

"Y…you can talk too?!"

"Oh, I forgot to tell you," Coco interjected. "I gave him a voice synthesizer using natural language processing. He can not only talk, but he's also got a bit of a brain, so don't think of him as just a dumb robot. He may very well surprise us down the road."

"Remarkable," Lucas expressed with amazement. "Isn't it!" Steve exclaimed.

"Max, that's…actually brilliant. It's fresh. It's what the industry needs. How did you…" Lucas trailed off as Max found a natural entrance for his answer.

"I've been learning from the best and analyzing a lot of data– petabytes of it, in fact. In fact, I am AGI–Artificial General Intelligence."

"What's that? Is that like AI squared?" Lucas asked.

"As a highly advanced android specialized in being at peak physical performance, suave, and smart. AGI allows me to master any task, from creative arts to scientific discovery, much like a human, although I have been programmed to focus on fitness excellence. AGI aims to generalize across domains, adapt, and learn with autonomy, which I can do. While I excel in a narrow field, AGI represents the potential for AI to understand, innovate, and interact across the full spectrum of human activities, posing profound ethical and societal questions. AGI embodies the future of AI, blurring lines between machine and human intellect."

Steve laughed as Lucas's face stayed in a perpetual state of bewilderment. "Looks like we've not only created the perfect athlete to represent thrivXR, but he's now apparently also our leading creative mind. It makes us pause and consider the role of AI in society and its potential to transcend being a mere tool or mimicry and become a source of inspiration and innovation in its own right.

This is the future, Lucas. Can you grasp the breadth of all of this?"

"It's nothing like we've seen before," Coco said. "Max isn't just a part of the team; he's leading us into completely new territory here."

From that point forward, Max would be a part of thrivXR and BeTells. His integration into the productions as a super dooper looper would make this former AI bot-turned-human android the key to the team's success. Surprise and innovation were hardcoded into Max Pozel. After all, he did surprise everyone by coming up with Maximum Positive. This modern Pinnochio would also be given a unique quirk that the gang hatched up.

"I knew I could count on you two," Lucas told Coco and Steve. "Thanks a million for helping bring my vision over the finish line. I foresee us achieving tremendous success with the help of Max. And this gives me an idea I'll share with you in that meeting at Escape Control Central we have coming up."

"Color me intrigued," Coco replied. "You will be."

"Lucas, you got that presentation ready?" "Almost, Steve."

"What's it about?" Coco asked.

"I'll keep it a surprise," Lucas returned. He wanted to make sure he did a little more polishing before he revealed the BeTells-focused presentation."

"A man of mystery. I like it," replied Coco with a smirk.

The trio broke their huddle, with Steve and Coco heading out.

"You want us to take Max with us, or are you going to hold onto him?" Steve asked.

"I think he'll stick with me for now. But given that he's got that AGI running, who knows what will happen? It seems Max may end up being able to bend reality to his will...and that gives me a brilliant idea for my looper." It was clear Lucas just had a *Eureka* moment.

"Sounds good; catch ya later," Steve replied.

* * * *

A few days later, Lucas called in the BeTells dream team for a meeting at the Escape Control Central for what would become pivotal for the entire production agenda.

"Ready to get started?" Steve Yabbs, one of the key investors for thrivXR, asked Lucas Disney. "We need to go ahead and solidify everyone's investments in this project–especially Y-Ali's and Yolanda Goldberg's."

Lucas, the owner of the BeTells Creative Reality TV agency and the thrivXR sports + fitness club, heard Steve's question yet was a bit apprehensive as something weighed on his mind. It involved Coco Oprahprada, of course.

Surrounded by short, neat stacks of folders, notebooks, and pieces of paper, Steve tried to bring Lucas back out of his demure state.

"Lucas? You ok, buddy?" he asked.

"Yes," Lucas replied with a sigh. "But I'm nervous about Coco. I just know she isn't going to understand the casting decisions, and she is going to be pissed."

"Well, just remember," Steve quickly retorted, attempting to be encouraging, "it's not *wha*t you say; it's *how* you say it. She'll be on board...trust me. I'll knock her down, build her back up, cut her loose, and she'll stand and deliver. You watch."

Steve was a natural at his chosen role in thrivXR and BeTells. However, his path to get here was not all sunshine and rainbows– mostly due to issues that stemmed from not wanting to take over the family business.

You see, Steve harbored intense anger at his grandfather, who had disdain for Steve's father. The issue Steve's grandfather had was that Steve's father did not want to go into the family business. There was a generational deal that he did not want to upkeep. After all, people change and have their own interests and goals, and they don't always match what their families want them to do.

The company was in the printing business. Steve's great-grandfather started the enterprise, passing it down to his son, who would become Steve's grandfather. When it came time to pass the baton to Steve's father, he refused. He wanted to do something else with his life, even though the business was booming thanks to a proprietary printing process Steve's great-grandfather invented. The company was highly innovative, enabling it to develop a flurry of patents similar to how microprocessor companies like Intel make smaller and smaller chips. Their technology made it possible for an authenticity verification process that proved to become more valuable over time as demand grew.

Even though Steve's father chose to go in a different direction than the family business, he had a knack for it and learned a lot about business through being a part of the company. This led him to develop excellent business acumen, which he took with him and imparted into his son. Steve followed in his father's footsteps and eventually left the family business as well, becoming exceedingly successful in his own right. His commitment to accept the wisdom his father imparted to him inspired his career that focused on the tech sector.

Lucas looked at Steve, exasperated and shuffling papers.

"I think I need a little bit more time to think about my presentation to her," Lucas affirmed.

"Well, you have about 30 seconds. I just saw her pull into the parking lot," Steve quickly shot back.

"Oh, great..." Lucas said while rolling his eyes.

The two of them looked out onto the thrivXR parking lot to see the ever-glamorous five-time Grammy winner Coco Oprahprada walking from her car towards the front door, with sunglasses adorning her face as her hair blew fabulously in the wind.

Tough, polished, professional. Sharp cheekbones sculpted natural face, bright eyes. Coco is known as "sparkly" in the talent industry not just because she emanates huge positive energy and beauty but those apt to be a fan experience inspiration and existential excitement in her presence. Stunning.

She is an investor in BeTells and an accomplished movie star client who was a year ahead of Lucas in high school. Lucas' parents, who owned and operated a talent agency, discovered Coco and launched her career. As she became one of the industry's most successful movie stars, Coco changed her representation to CAA. Later, she agreed to work with Lucas' talent agency, BeTells, and take an operational role to grow a media empire. At the Vanity Fair afterparty of the 2022 Oscars, when Coco won her third Best Actor Award, Coco saw and connected with Steve, who has invested in starting up thrivXR as a corporate client for BeTells.

Just before Coco entered Escape Control Central (Lucas' offices), Lucas saw her approaching through the one-way glass wall. As she approached, an astounding and turbulent prismatic bubble four inches wide reflected off the one-way mirror and appeared face-high and just three inches in front of Coco's left cheekbone. Coco couldn't help but stare, mesmerized at the bubble as the AR projector shot the image from just above the doorbell. As soon as the bubble captured Coco's complete attention, it exploded into a five-foot tall, beautiful, lush plant with captivating flowers undulating in the wind and emitting a soothing rhythmic tune. Coco was moved, surprised, and delighted. As she moved forward, fully enthralled by and focused on the illusion, she bumped her head right into the one-way mirror glass door. Steve and Lucas shared a muffled snicker as Coco sauntered into Escape Control Central.

"Since when do we have a door here?" Coco asked, motioning with her thumb as she walked in.

"Ehh...there's always been a door there, Coco..." Lucas replied.

Taking a mere sniff in response, she sauntered around the table, sizing up the nearby whiteboard with her eyes before elegantly, yet firmly, taking a seat.

"It's been a while, Steve. Are you ruler of the metaverse yet?" she razzed.

"Good one, Coco. Glad we're on the team together to launch BeTells. I'm going to hit up the boxing robot downstairs in a bit. Care to join me?" he asked her with a bit of a boastful tone.

"I'm down for that for sure," she winked before turning her attention to Lucas.

Steve interjected pointedly, "I'm here to tell you that we will be unleashing the power of the force of nature through the talent agency platform."

Coco, impressed with Steve's bravado, cocked her head to listen. Lucas stared wide-eyed, not knowing what to expect.

Steve slouched with a heavy heart. "Years ago, I bid and lost the Salvator Mundi at Christie's Auction House. I really felt like I was going to be able to be a part of history with this acquisition. It was astounding to me that I was in a position to actually compete. I have always studied the creation of sensations and have been fascinated by how they actually happen. Leonardo Da Vinci was among a handful of talented and accomplished artists of his time, yet his Mona Lisa has become the most famous piece of all time. Why is that? Well, I'll tell you why." Steve paused for a moment before continuing.

"A skilled and ambitious craftsman earned the single most important and essential element needed to service the Louvre in Paris. And that single most important element...was trust. When Leonardo DaVinci painted the Mona Lisa, he had a personal understanding of the tissue, muscle structure, and bone structure that underlies facial expressions because he, like Michelangelo, dissected human cadavers. This visceral, tactile knowledge enabled him to create a visage that was so magnetic to anybody who could see it at the time. No paintings had ever embodied the lifelike and ethereal breathtaking presence like the Mona Lisa at the time Da Vinci painted her. Also, Mona Lisa was a high-level socialite, so people were fascinated to see her then. Once the painting was stolen in 1911, it became a huge worldwide story. Then, years later, the guilty thief was caught, the painting was recovered, and it was restored to its home at the Louvre, and worldwide everybody wanted to see it, so that's how it became and remains the most famous painting of all time. That's the *only* reason that the da Vinci's Salvator Mundi could fetch a record-breaking price of $450M at auction."

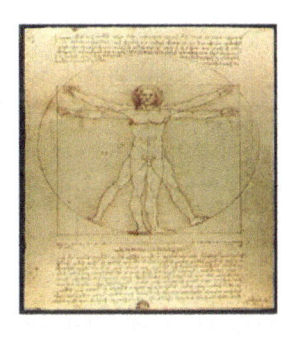

Leonardo da Vinci dissected more than 30 human corpses to learn human anatomy.

Steve Yabbs, early investor in Apple.

The subject of Mona Lisa by Leonardo da Vinci was the socialite Lisa Gehrardini del Giocondo.

In 2017, Salvator Mundi, the painting by Leonardo da Vinci, sold for over $450 million at Christie's auction house in New York City.

At Escape Control Central, you could hear a pin drop, as Steve excitedly divulged this art history that intertwined with his personal failure to make this acquisition, "Knowledge, at its very essence, can only be a justified and true belief because, ultimately, we are confronted by the chicken and the egg problem. How do we know what we know? Heisenberg's uncertainty principal plays bare the truth that anything you measure is impacted by the fact that you are measuring it. Famously, Baron Munchausen is the centerpiece of a myth where he is on horseback trapped in a quagmire of mud. In the myth, he impossibly escapes by taking both of his hands and hoisting himself and the horse by pulling his hair straight up. So, my most special gift accomplishes the impossible by making something from nothing to create a sensation …not that anybody is nothing, but that's a gift I have–how to maximize talent. That's how the whole Y-Ali sensation got started. I saw three of her videos and knew that she had the passion, tenacity, and drive to become the biggest worldwide YouTube sensation that the world has ever seen." Coco and Lucas nodded confirming they were interested and went with the flow without totally understanding what Steve was saying.

Steve had a special relationship with Y-Ali. Yet, they both kept it secret…for a time. Although nobody in the room knew how deep their ties went, Steve was instrumental in Y-Ali's success, coaching her and providing her with guidance to honor her legend from very early in her career. He wanted to put feathers in her cap and cash in her pocket because of his strong desire to help her get to the next level. He saw her extraordinary potential when few others did. Their mentor-coach relationship formed a strong bond between them, and while they did not reveal their professional relationship yet, they knew it would happen soon enough.

Back in the Escape Control Central conference room, with a faux serious sardonic news broadcaster tone, Steve shouted out, "Life force! We start with the New England Medical Journal. BAM! It's prestigious…it's high level…it's the New England Medical Journal!" He then paused for dramatic effect, leaving Coco and Lucas deeply intrigued. Steve, straining to maintain a serious demeanor, continued on.

"So, we could start a multi-decade research funding grant request campaign to finally prove and validate my theory that…" Steve, who struggled at this point to maintain composure, began to surrender to strange facial gestures before continuing on to say, " regular

application of fresh semen to women's breasts delays sag and improves perkiness."

Lucas slapped the table, infuriated, before shouting out, "I honestly don't know how to respond to you. I mean, I know you're brilliant and successful...and I just...I just...don't know."

Coco's eye roll faded into a soft, controlled chuckle that she successfully stifled before busting out with infectious guffaws, leading to the group having difficulty getting back on track without laughing. Finally, Coco redirected the conversation to Lucas. The two have quite the history.

You see, Lucas was the quarterback of his varsity football team during his time at the prestigious St. Mark's High School–the same school Owen Wilson went to. Since he attended one of the best college prep schools in the nation, he could easily get into Stanford, after which he came back to Dallas in a very innovative way, following many trajectories in high school and throughout college. An important thing to note about Lucas is that he was a very curious explorer of Bounty.

Coco and Lucas have known each other since they were kids and had become close friends in adulthood. Coco had even seen Lucas get married and divorced while she stayed single. They were aware of one another in grade school, especially through interactions on the schoolyard. However, they didn't really get close until high school, where their proximity given they were both in the same honors classes, led to greater natural interaction. However, they were always on their best behavior around each other, even while having developed a passionate attraction for one another, which was ultimately left unactualized. At Homecoming, each of them had their own date but had an unspoken acknowledgment of a deep, mutual attraction. During these earlier years, they experienced a defining moment in how they understood themselves.

During high school, paths started diverging before coalescing again. Coco became a model and movie star, at first represented locally. This early rise to stardom meant she did not really get to experience her senior year of high school the way most teens do because she was working much of the time and had ended up establishing several major studio multimedia blockbusters in the metaverse and in movies.

In 2023, Lucas graduated from high school at St. Mark's. Given Coco's glamorous LA life, she had spent pretty much all of senior year on set in LA, rather than making memories with her friends at her all-girls school called Hockaday in Dallas. The movies she was making senior year came out two years later, in 2025. She ended up being propelled to superstardom at the young age of 20. Even throughout all of her early career success, and despite living halfway across the country, Coco always measured anyone she met up to Lucas. They did end up having a few interactions here and there during these years and were acutely aware of each other's growing reputation.

Lucas was just as motivated as Coco, which is something else the two of them shared. Lucas at first played soccer and football but ultimately gave up soccer to go on and become a tennis champion. He was a local favorite. Under these auspices, he bought thrivXR. Having achieved business success over nine years at this point while in school, including having a home painting business where he painted his classmates' houses, he was able to fund his deep interests like going to film festivals and pursuing his parents' talent agency.

Given they were involved in the talent arena of the film industry, Lucas' parents were involved in Sundance, Tribeca, and Cannes film festivals. They tried to strategically hit those festivals with different initiatives, some films getting submitted into all three while others were geared towards a particular crowd. Throughout grade school, Lucas had this scene as a backdrop since his parents took him with them around, and he got to know everyone in the film community and understood the industry from a talent agency business perspective. It's also probably a good idea for you to know that Lucas had a special relationship with Coco partly due to his father having helped sponsor her.

In fact, one day after football practice, Coco had lingered after dropping off her friend Marnie Ericjohnson for cheerleading tryouts. Lucas, transfixed by the strumming of Coco's acoustic guitar, caught a sight that stirred within him from that time forward, changing him from a boy to a man. Coco, lightly singing, perched comfortably on the end of bleacher, facing away from the field, crooned Moon River by Johnny Mercer,

"..... Two drifters off to see the world. There's such a lot of world to see. We're after the same rainbow's end

waitin' round the bend, my Huckleberry friend Moon river and me"

Lucas unconsciously ambled over from behind, whispered his confession in Coco's ear, "I'm captivated."

"Yes, well, to me, the tune is all about following your heart. That's how I hope to live."

Feeling his presence and recognizing his voice, after letting the last guitar notes hang in the air, Coco looked over her shoulder to stare deeply into Lucas' warm, brown eyes, with her brilliant, enchanting smile, charming cheeks, and laughing eyes and her hair blowing in the light, forgiving breeze her words spoken through a sigh in response to Lucas' confession.

Lucas whispers audibly, "Well, in that case, I'm certain you'll arrive somewhere you belong."

His sweat dripping from his brow down his face, and the heat of his body nudged through the breeze to blanket Coco's shoulder. Having weathered the Dallas heat during late August football practice, pheromones pumping from both his physical exertion from practice but also from having shared his nice reflection with Coco, Lucas feels light, happy, vulnerable and strong and lucky and shy and bold and brand new and inspired and enraptured with Coco's all-encompassing natural beauty.

There are times when a split second, the thinnest of slices of reality, an immediate and expert decision may change the course of human history. This was one of those far-reaching, ripple effect, nuclear reaction type of moments. At this very moment, with a knowing sparkle in his eye, Lucas the boy, accepted the gravity of his manhood like a heavy trophy. But in the very same instant of acceptance, he gave it away, actively denying his impulse to reach out to touch Coco's hand or maybe even her cheek, to evolve their friendship and acquiesce to the palpable roar of their undeniable mutual attraction and deep connection.

With the resolve to connect Coco with his father for representation, this life-defining moment cut an alternative path entirely in sacrifice to his duty to family needs and ambitions. Lucas' sophisticated and nuanced and professional appreciation of Coco's natural raw beauty and talent would prove to rock, spice and imprint generations and generations of fans who would ultimately become obsessed with Coco Oprahprada, a name that Luke's father would later help Coco to adopt.

"Yes, but will I have a name?" Coco craves to know.

"Well, sometimes you just have to wait around to find out," Lucas hears himself say through a knowing, happy smile.

With that backstory wrapped up, let's see what's happening back in Escape Control Central...

"Alright, let's get right to it and talk about this Buff Pepper character you've created. He intrigues me. What's the name of the woman he's pining for?" she asked pointedly.

"Well, just to keep it simple..." Lucas started off nervously, anticipating Coco's reaction, "I thought her name should be Coco...Coco Twain."

"Seriously?" she fired back, stunned at what she had just heard.

24 ELVIS SWIFTY

Code of Bounty
My Worth, My Soulmate & the XR Revolution

Best XR Money Making Book of All Time Seller

—GAMSON—

Lucas Elvis Disney

with a forward by 3 time Acadamy Award Winning Best Actor
Coco Opraprada

The Bible of NIL Sponsorships

"Killing me softly... As you might imagine, I felt so vulnerable when Buff presented the proposed book cover pictured above to the whole team including Coco at Escape Control Central." Lucas

CODE of BOUNTY

The XR Revolution:
Thriving in the Future of Business with Authentic Artist Self Replacement

Lucas Elvis Disney

with a forward by 3 time Acadamy Award Winning Best Actor
Coco Opraprada

The Bible of NIL Sponsorships

Best #1 XR Money Making Book of All Time Seller

"While I found Max's proposed cover (pictured above) compelling, the team felt that we needed to strike a clear cord with athletes, content creators and fitness influencers. Of course, Max's vision to deliver 'Authentic Artist Self Replacement" was both well intentioned and completely infuriating to Y-Ali. Max's idea is to alleviate artists of the need to actually be involved with creating, performing and promoting their art once they imprint an indelible and intrinsically unique art body on the AI droid. Max envisions providing ongoing revenue streams to the artist without continued effort by the artist. For many decades, artists have benefited from many forms of production, recording, performing and promotion technologies. This leveling up by AI is an unstoppable evolution." Lucas

"Why not? It's a cool name. You'll like her character, I promise," he reassured her. "It's like this, Coco. You see, Coco Twain was a year ahead of Buff, and Buff's folks represented Coco Twain."

With a raised eyebrow, she started putting two and two together. "Sounds dangerously familiar, Lucas. Isn't that just like you and me?" she asked.

"Yeah, well, that's where the similarity stops because I composed a song and AI-genned up a music video about electric bikes and…well, we didn't have electric bikes when we were young," Lucas told her.

Coco smirked with amusement. "Interesting. So, can I see it?"

Lucas grabbed a remote off the conference table and pushed a button to turn on the flat-panel TV on the wall. After another click of the remote, a video started playing at near full volume. The opening scene introduced 64 competitors on electric bikes, paired up in couples and synchronized and choreographed by bike type as the *Electric Bike* music video's lyrics are sung with gusto.

Coco watched the scene playing out before her eyes with excitement and determination to be a part of it. This was her jam, after all. She couldn't help but start humming along every time the chorus repeated *"Electric bike, electric bike, electric bike"* as any musically adept creative would feel compelled to do.

As she continued to watch, Coco was getting a barrage of ideas for how she could take on the idea of electric bikes and be their champion. After all, she had been fascinated by them for years and had amassed the most notable collection. She knew all the different makes and models worth knowing about, helping her friends pick the right electric bike for them.

With this almost unusual love affair with electric bikes being the essential element of her early work on social media as an electric bike enthusiast on YouTube and infused in her private life (paparazzi relish catching her riding the various types of electric bikes in her collection), she even started brainstorming innovative improvements to them, like integrated force fields by 2026 that would have a sort of crash cushion pillow effect going. Sure, it seems out of this world, yet she came across some Top Secret classified documents from an Unacknowledged Special Access Program (USAP) out of NASA that she had been working on manipulating the polarization of electromagnetic fields. She wanted to be a household name when revolutionizing electric bikes.

Lucas pressed a button on the remote to turn off the screen, turning towards Coco to see her reaction, who was now exceedingly engaged and hyped and even a little bossy with what she said next.

"I want to sing the 'Electric Bike' song as a solo. Use your imagination, Lucas. Make it happen," she demanded. It was clear to her that the AI-generated version of Electric Bikes was completely on-brand as being a BeTells production, and she was determined to make it a stellar success...with the help of her artistic passion, of course.

"It's not quite like that. Every creation is delivered by a muse and is on loan from an angel, hence the Bracelets and Chains allegory that you like so well," he retorted.

"Bracelets and Chains. I agree; that's tight. Can you let me get more clarity on how they work into the system?" she asked, feeling a surge of creative energy, sensing her core self has already known but craves to refine a foggy memory. She made sure to be all ears after getting hyped by the Electric Bikes music video.

"Well," Lucas said, "here's the added context to know about this idea. Upon registration, each BeTells Champion will be connected with one of you BeTells–Yolanda, Steve, Buff, Coco Twain, Max, Y- Ali, you, or myself. After that, our Champions must choose either a Bracelet or Chain. This is Steve's brainchild, so I should let him explain it more." Lucas looked over to Steve and motioned for him to explain away.

"Right, so here's the deal," Steve started explaining, "This ecosphere is straight up transcendental, and to encapsulate that, we can think of the symbolism and the acknowledgment of two sides of the same coin of the ecosphere. On one side, we have the Shadow Self, while on the other is the Authentic Self. These are two states of mind that we all experience at different points. Overall, it's a progression and ascent, but we all go back and forth...sometimes two steps forward and one step back, two steps back and one step forward, three steps back and one step forward, and so on. Ultimately, when we are more lucid and conscious, we continue the spiral toward self- actualization, just like in Maslow's Hierarchy of Needs."

"This has substance," Coco cooly acknowledged.

"It sure does," Steve replied, "but having the acknowledgment of your creative genius means a lot."

"So, I'm seeing this gel with my mantra from Pablo Picasso, 'The meaning of life is to find your gift. The purpose of life is to give it away,' which I have evolved my understanding to mean that throughout our lives, we can quench ourselves within one, two, or maybe three, five, or 10-year cycles where we uncover synergistic gifts. But, just like the universe and astrophysics mirror quantum physics in a way, we can experience micro moment-to-moment realizations of our unique gifts."

"Sure, and did you get that from my doctoral thesis?" Steve wondered.

"Ha! Nope, but this is totally on-brand for you, Steve," she replied.

"You intuit me well, and we are definitely tracking," he responded. "So anyway, let me explain where the Bracelets and Chains come in. The Shadow Self is rooted in our human and animal instincts. Think unconscious shadow aspects, including the anima and animus, as Jungian psychology explains. The Authentic Self is expressed when someone is in the flow state, in the zone, and in the moment, and their gift is shared through the ecosphere and into the world. To explain it in as condensed a way as I can, the Shadow Self is a Goer, while the Authentic Self is a Thriver. A Chain is a symbol for the Shadow Self, which is compelled, while a Bracelet is a symbol for the Authentic Self, which is inspired. A Bracelet represents the Higher Self that is value-driven and value-directed and on a proactive and intentional mission. A Chain represents the more primal nature that wants to get shit done, hustle and grind, and go hard. When a Champion comes into BeTells, we want to ask them whether they are choosing the chain or the bracelet. The essence of all this is that a Champion may choose to switch between the two to match their vibe and trajectory and what they're resonating with at any moment."

"Yes, indeed..." continued Coco slowly, drawing out her words in a thoughtful, deep state of consciousness. "So, I've evolved a sense of vibing out where people are at in those regards. It's not so much an either/or analysis as it is a preponderance and most likely a comfortable feeling. Most like both Elvis and the Beatles, but at any given consciousness cycle, they will have a much more intense proclivity to be enamored with one over the other."

Simultaneously, in reflective harmony, Steve and Coco, staring at one another, saying, "Elvis is chain state and Beatles conjure bracelets."

Lucas, not surprised, but surprised that he's not surprised at this astounding, metaphysical "click" that he just witnessed, tapped into a powerful, synergistic energy that inspired him to contribute, adding, "...or with Drake you'd be chain and Swifties are bracelets. So, it follows that during conversation with others, you are either in the instinctual realm of thinking of what you will say next or are more likely to open your consciousness with deep listening."

"Yeah, listeners want bracelets," Steve intoned while Coco nodded. "You either have distilled out your personal value system and written it down, or you vibe out your path more instinctually. I've shared mine with both of you," Lucas added.

"So, in that case, you'd be tilting towards the bracelet," Coco shared in a solemn tone of deep admiration.

"OK, now I'm going to take a hard left turn into an area I am more familiar with. I'd like to be cast as Max Pozel's girlfriend...what was her name again? Was it Delilah?" she asked him. However, Lucas confidently shook his head in a slight "No" as a response to her question.

"Y-Ali's star is rising. I had to give that role to Y-Ali. It's actually perfect for her," Lucas told her. It was clear that Coco was becoming quite infuriated at the news.

"So, what does that mean? Am I on the way out?" she asked with exasperation. "I want a recurring spotlight!" she added.

"I know, I know...and we have that for you, actually. Just trust me

on this, Coco," Lucas responded. However, that didn't stop her from glaring like darts at him.

"Trust me, as your agent," he added, wanting to reassure her that everything would work out in the best way possible. Coco took a deep breath, relaxing and cocking her head to hear out what Lucas had to say. He never let her down, so she decided to give his idea a chance. You already know about my business acumen, successes over the years, and philosophy. You know that I will stop at nothing to create the most compelling sports and fitness company of the 21st century by leading the world's shift to gamify sports and fitness with XR...and putting on dramatic and comedic mock weddings while we're at it. So, I believe your stature will best serve as a guiding light to both your fans and artists alike," Lucas said.

"I'm listening," Coco replied.

"It's a talk show format called *Sunglasses with Coco*, which will become the ultimate beacon for fashion and art–worldwide. Believe it or not, it was actually Y-Ali's idea," Lucas told her proudly.

"OK. You've got my ear. Tell me more," she prompted.

Lucas cleared his throat before giving her a response, telling her, "I will...soon. Currently, Y-Ali is coming by here to discuss joining this project. Glad you're here too."

Coco was doing her best to feign off the boredom that was quickly settling in, doing what she always did in these situations: take out her phone and scroll through her Instagram feed. Lucas got an idea, so he started typing out intently on his laptop, not bothering to look up at Coco. He suddenly stopped to tell her vital information he had forgotten earlier.

"Oh, by the way, Steve has confirmed with none other than Yolanda Goldberg. We'll call her in a bit as well," he shared.

"Wow..." Coco replied, noticeably impressed.

Steve leaned forward in his chair to get closer to Lucas to interject as if on cue. "So, tell me the story with Y-Ali again."

"She was a YouTube star. Scratch that–IS a YouTube star. It's complicated. In any case, she's smart and positive, and she's just what we need. Here, check this out." Lucas pressed a button on the conference table to bring up YouTube on the screen. Once it loaded, he pulled up Y-Ali's YouTube channel and started playing a video as the two continued to chat. The video began with a dramatic voiceover by the YouTube sensation.

"In the future, everyone will be famous for 15 minutes!"

"Wow. 3.4 billion subscribers?" Steve asked in shock.

"Yeah, isn't that something?" She made herself famous for singing in her authentic voice with auto-tune. Her mantra is 'be your true self,' he said, using air quotes for emphasis. "She would make a great coach for our BeTells champions on how to build an online following."

"Sure, sounds like it, but didn't we talk about Yolanda filling that role, though? You know, she already ran a few ideas by us like Bracelets and Chains that fold right in with the competition. And her philanthropy. She just brings so much to this project," Steve said.

Lucas tagged onto what Steve shared, adding his two cents. "Yolanda is a legend, for sure. Why don't we just have Yolanda and Y-Ali work on that part of the project together?" he asked.

"We could...that would be interesting, alright. Yep, let's do that," Steve replied.

Just then, the larger-than-life Y-Ali entered the room, looking fresh and smiling, giving off a funky-cool, yet tasteful, vibe.

"Hi everyone! Y-Ali is in the house!"

Lucas flashed her a big smile, replying, "Why yes, she is! Y-Ali, meet Steve Yabbs. Steve, this is the amazing Y-Ali."

Steve enthusiastically stood up from his chair, making his way over to Y-Ali to shake her hand. "Pleasure, Y-Ali."

"Steve Yabbs...I used to see you all over the web," Y-Ali responded.

"Well," he started off, "we certainly have that in common, don't we? I've stepped back from those other ventures for now and have been pouring myself into BeTells Agency and working with my friends Lucas and Coco on the thrivXR TriBoxalon competition. You could say that I'm all in."

"Speaking of going all in," Lucas interjected, "I think this is a good time to lay down the culture constitution I have developed for the content that BeTells will create. The foundational DNA binds the production together and will be the key to its success. Competition, charity, and art combine to fuel the essence of the BeTells Creative Reality TV Agency, which explosively combusts into a roaring flame of soulful, healthy goodness, flickering with playful and fun flashes of light and being grounded in reality. It will be the North Star for Tone, Sentiment, and Gravitas of Content, if you will."

"And these core elements are going to help people become self- actualized wealth generators, right?" Steve asked Lucas.

"Right on the money, Steve," Lucas shot back. "These will help the reality of financial independence for fitness influencers, life coaches, personal trainers, actors, producers, and musicians. It's time for people who fall into these walks of life to materialize their wealth on the go, thriving in their art and life. You see, creative reality happens increasingly in the *moment* as you become the star of your career. So, laying down the groundwork becomes the release you're looking for on a daily basis, which becomes financial income that increases every year. You are growing ongoing revenue streams designed to develop a 10-year wealth creation balance sheet with the vision of creating generational wealth."

"I love how you think big; I've always liked that about you," Steve told him.

"Thanks, Steve. I don't see any other way to live," he replied. However, Lucas suddenly turned pale and looked horrified. He knew that he had forgotten something! Quickly, he scurried over to Coco, who was throwing one dagger after the other at him with her eyes. Thankfully, he cleverly figured out how to neutralize the tenseness in the room, which was thick enough that you could cut it with a knife.

"I'm sorry, but you know how passionate I get about this. Y- Ali...this is the one and only Coco Oprahprada. Among her dozens of amazing attributes and accomplishments, Coco is another major investor in BeTells Creative Agency, and she will play a major role in producing the TriBoxAlon competition through thrivXR," he quickly said before giving out a deep exhale. His plan worked. Coco slightly narrowed her eyes before nodding her head at Y-Ali, which sent the message that she was wiser, more experienced, and had the ear of both Lucas and Steve.

"Nice to meet you, Coco," Y-Ali said while popping her chewing gum. "Yeah...can we talk about that thrivXR competition? You know I'm not a major jock, right? I'm an *en-ter-tain-er*, "she enunciated. "Do you really see me kicking someone's butt on the boxing robot?" she added.

"Not at all," Lucas replied. "We see you in a completely different role. This competition is so much more than that! We will work with 64 super-talented influencers who will audition in a dramatic comedy role as part of the competition. As I mentioned, they're called Champions–32 women and 32 men. These fitness influencers will come to the XR competition for a TriboxAlon, pay a fee, do a double looper, and audition by reading a script where they predefined roles in our super-duper double looper. The top 16 guys and girls get to select who to do the scenes with, and everyone will then choose a charity to support. I've run the numbers and have come up with the perfect distribution model: 40% goes to the fitness influencer, another 40% goes to their charity of choice, 15% goes to the company, and 5% is given to the sponsor or celebrity host."

Making sure everyone was following, Lucas let his words sink in.

"The other side of this is the employees," he added. "I'm really going meta on this one. Everyone who's part of the staff will need to always maintain character. This means all employees will be required to maintain the demeanor and persona of one of the characters within our production. There will be multiple employees serving as different characters depending on their scheduling. So, when fitness influencers enter the BeTells facility, they will be greeted by none other than Yolanda Goldberg in the lobby and connected with a member of BeTells."

Coco, ever the skeptic with eyebrows raised, leaned forward. "Hold up. You mean to tell me we're going to play ourselves... as characters? In some sort of meta-theatrical performance art?"

"Exactly!" Lucas beamed as if he'd just revealed a magician's final act. Coco couldn't help but laugh. "Well, that's one way to avoid hiring actors, I guess."

The room buzzed with a mix of amusement and intrigue. Sensing the moment's ripe potential, Lucas dove deeper into the vision. "And it doesn't stop there. Imagine a competition where fitness influencers aren't just hitting the gym—they're battling it out on virtual flying machines, duking it out with boxing robots, racing on omnidirectional treadmills, and leading their avatars to victory. All while amassing an army of followers online and honing their theatrical prowess. It's not just a competition; it's a spectacle."

Steve, always eager to add clarity, chimed in. "And by 'you,' he means you and Yolanda," nodding towards Y-Ali.

"Wait, Yolanda Goldberg?" Y-Ali's voice dripped with disbelief, her previous amusement fading. "As in, the Yolanda Goldberg?"

Lucas, oblivious to the brewing storm, nodded enthusiastically. "Yes! Have you two crossed paths before?"

Y-Ali's response was a mixture of sarcasm and genuine annoyance. "Crossed paths? More like she practically bulldozed me at the awards show last year. She threw shade my way so hard it could've eclipsed the sun. And now you want me to work with her? She's practically the antithesis of everything online entertainment stands for."

Steve, ever the mediator, attempted to smooth things over. "Ah, but remember, Yolanda is a titan in her field—a blend of business acumen and philanthropic prowess. Right, Lucas?"

The room was thick with tension, uncertainty, and a palpable sense of excitement. This wasn't just another project; it was shaping up to be a clash of titans, a meeting of minds, and perhaps the most dramatic and comedic endeavor they'd ever undertaken. The BeTells project was no longer just a competition; it was a battleground for old school versus new school, with Y-Ali and Yolanda Goldberg at the heart of the drama.

"Yes, and we're very fortunate to have her on the team with her platform of Maximizing One's Legend Through Charity."

"And if you're not careful," Coco added, "you just might learn something from her." Just then, Lucas' phone rang.

"Here, she is calling us now. Right on time. Punctuality makes me all squishy inside."

Coco rolled her eyes at Lucas' corniness while he pressed the large button on the Escape Control Central conference table to answer the video call. Sure enough, Yolanda Goldberg appeared on the screen and was larger than life, in exactly the grand dame style she would always wish to be seen, with her perfectly coiffed hair and professionally applied makeup. She flashed the entire room a controlled, demure smile.

"Hello dah-lings," Yolanda doled out to the room.

"Yolanda!" Lucas exclaimed. "Wonderful to see you again! Thanks for taking the time to join us. From the looks of things, you're not in your office."

"I'm not," she replied. "I'm sitting in a quaint little bistro in Aspen. I'm here for a few days with my assistants while we wrap up another project."

"Well, we're over the moon that you'll join our project here at BeTells," Lucas informed her. "You're a legend on many levels." He then shot a glance at the others in the room, realizing he should re-introduce them to her. "Oh, and you remember Steve Yabbs and Coco Oprahprada, right?" he asked her. True to his style, Steve waved at the screen with goofy admiration.

"Good to see you again, Yolanda," replied Coco.

Lucas gestured to Y-Ali, saying, "...and may I introduce you to Y-Ali."

Yolanda moved in closer to the screen, with her nose seemingly making a run for it into Escape Control Central, which made everyone shrink back a bit. "Yes," she went on, "I believe we've met. Was that before or after that most unfortunate incident on YouTube?"

Clearly, Y-Ali was peeved at the remark, leading Lucas to quickly jump in to keep the conversation from becoming heated. The last thing anyone wanted was a verbal brawl going down at a moment when fostering collaboration was the goal.

"Well, you know this business, Yolanda. Sometimes, a few bumps in the road make a person's career even stronger. That's what this thrivXR competition is all about–doing what you do best, building a following, helping others along the way..." Yolanda cut Lucas off before he could finish.

"Yes, yes, I know. And I've already told you to count me in," she said.

"And we're excited to pair up you and Y-Ali..." Steve started saying before Yolanda started talking over him, raising her eyebrows at his statement.

"OH, REAL-LY?"

Steve continued nervously, but he knew he was treading on thin ice at that point. He continued, "...to help the competitors hone their public image and learn the importance of giving back through charity."

Lucas came in with the assist, saying, "We really can't think of a more dynamic duo than you and Y-Ali, Yolanda. Like you, y-Ali brings a refreshing authenticity to everything she does." He then turned to Y-Ali, telling her, "And Y-Ali, the energy you bring to this project is fantastic. We can't wait to see what you and Yolanda do together!"

Y-Ali finally remembered her manners, even though they were a bit forced, and replied, "Yes."

"I've got to go." Yolanda chimed in. "My assistant is motioning that my plane is ready at the airport."

"OK, Yolanda–great to see you, and thanks for the call! We'll be in touch!" Lucas said before she hopped off the call. Coco and Steve just managed to wave at the screen before it went black.

"Alright! That went well, didn't it?" Steve asked the room.

"I'm still not understanding how you want me to team up with Yolanda," Y-Ali told Lucas.

"It will all come together in time as this thing grows," he assured her.

"Aren't you going to tell her about Delilah?" Coco asked Lucas.

"Delilah? Who's Delilah? You mean you're making me work with even more judgmental dinosaurs?" Y-Ali asked, sounding more flustered by the second.

Lucas chuckled before saying, "No, Y-Ali...we want you to have a role in this production as well–as Delilah, who is Max Poz's girlfriend. He's the ultimate competitor at thrivXR. You know the type. He breaks all the records on the machines, sings, drives a great car, is an athlete, recording artist, and all that."

"Is he hot?" Y-Ali asked, making it almost sound as if it would be a dealbreaker if he weren't.

"Don't worry, Y-Ali," Coco laughed. "We've made sure he's hot."

"If you have me playing a role in the production, it sounds like I won't have time to work with Yolanda." Y-Ali informed Lucas.

"Not true...there's definitely time for you two to work together," Lucas returned back. "You'll see. It's going to be epic."

"If you say so. I'm sure I'm needed for something way beyond sports. The influencers you're looking for need to have it all–the moves, the voice, *a video presence*, right? I will help with that."

"That's why we're glad to have you on the team, Y-Ali!" Lucas said. "Oh! By the way...there's something I wanted to show you," he added. As he had done earlier, he picked up the TV remote to turn on the screen to show the *Electric Bike* video. He intended to impress Y-Ali with the production and then say a few words about it, but Coco cut him off before he could get a single word in.

"Steve already promised me I could be the lead singer for the music video," Coco blurted out, adding, "...an AI-generated music video about electric bikes, of all things, couldn't be more my thing, you know?"

It became clear to everyone in the room that Y-Ali took offense to the condescending way Coco expressed herself.

"Are you telling me THAT is an AI-generated video?!" she yelled out. "Uh, yeah...and?" Coco replied.

"NOT a fan...there, I said it. Sorry, y'all!" Y-Ali retorted, clearly infuriated by the concept.

"Let's all take a moment to get centered and consider both perspectives here," Lucas said, trying to calm the strengthening tempest forming within the room. "I'm sure we can come up with a scenario where the two of you both get what you want," he added.

"Lucas, you know I think you're a creative genius, but AI-generated just isn't my jam, ya know?" Y-Ali told him.

"I totally get it. This is really new tech, and I know it may take some getting used to, and..." Lucas started saying before getting cut off by Y-Ali.

"...and I want to do my own thing by stamping out AI. You know...bringing the fresh, real, and raw to the people to inspire them to create their bounty and self-actualize their way to wealth and all of that good good," she said. "I got it! I could call it AI STAMPOUT that's a real-world production written and produced by yours truly."

Lucas contemplated the idea, remembering that he needed to act as both a mediator and leader. "Alright, I think I know what to do," he said. "Coco, you can sing for the AI-generated version while you get the right to produce and write a non-AI version of Electric Bike, Y- Ali. Then, we can do some A/B testing and see which one is received more favorably by a sample size of our target audience. Sounds good?" he asked the two of them.

"Yeah, that's fine with me. I already know which one the winner will be," Coco stated matter-of-factly.

"Yeah...mine!" Y-Ali shot back. It was clearly a bit frosty between the two for the time being. "Well, I have to go now," she stated decisively.

"OK. We'll be in touch soon. In the meantime, 'Be authentic!' Lucas told her.

"Very funny," Y-Ali replied before leaving Escape Control Central. The trio all looked at each other before shrugging their shoulders. They knew that this was just how Y-Ali was, but she was a creative genius, so they accepted it as part of her process and charm.

While Steve, Lucas, and Coco stuck around in Escape Control Central to map out more of the epic production they have been working on, Y-Ali found her way downtown, walking briskly down a mostly empty sidewalk. She was clearly irritated, given that she was frantically shaking her hand while speaking to no one in particular.

"Yolanda? YOLANDA?! Why do I have to work with HER?" she asked the universe.

Y-Ali continued to march toward her apartment with the determination of a hurricane, her anger swirling around her like the fierce winds that precede a destructive storm. When she finally got home, she plopped heavily onto her couch and whipped out her phone to angrily scroll her favorite social media feed.

Meanwhile, back at Escape Control Central, after Lucas, Coco, and Steve wrapped up their meeting with Y-Ali and Yolanda, they started shifting gears, with Steve standing up and grabbing his laptop bag on his way out the door. Lucas was already clicking and clacking away on his laptop while Coco looked at him quizzically.

"I'm outta here for now," Steve told the room. "See ya, Steve," Coco replied.

<u>GUIDING LIGHT MANTRA CHAPTER 1:</u>

I will follow my curiosity to unlock the value of the forces of evolution, innovation and creativity in my life.

Chapter Two

Moments of Meaning

"I want somebody to love."

"*Who is Max Poz?*" Those four words, which Coco knew to be genius, written in chicken scratch on the whiteboard in the Escape Control Central conference room, tormented her. Why would Lucas wildly jump out of his office chair to write that?

Standing with arms folded and showing a bit of pensive confusion, Coco studied the whiteboard before letting out a dramatic exhale.

"Well, I read what you've put together so far for the script, but I don't understand exactly. Is Max Pozel our member? A movie? Or a live competition? I don't get it."

Being an investor in the BeTells Creative Reality TV Agency, Coco threw her weight around when it mattered. Her major role as executive producer of the thrivXR TriBox-alon competitions had evolved into talent management and even production assistant. As she directed a shotgun of questions at Lucas, she already knew his answer would be like a seven-layer cake.

"Well…" Lucas said, eyes lighting up with excitement, "All of those, really." Becoming deeply intrigued and showing her silent approval, Coco let Lucas continue with his train of thought, which was now full steam ahead.

"So, we've got our guy! We'll cast Max Pozel, who has a real shot at winning. He'll be our Charlie–like in Willy Wonka, but it'll be more of a meritocracy–he's got to be at least a contender for a real competition. Really; it's like Ready Player One, and he's like Wade Owen Watts who…" Lucas paused, "was born August 12, 2029."

Coco let out an exasperated sigh. She became more animated as she got ready to unleash one of her epic rants.

"What are you talking about?!" she exclaimed. "It's 2028 right now, and we're talking about a tournament or movie to be shot this year in six months from the time we sign a sponsor. ViralSponsors.com says they can finish it two weeks from the day you choose a sponsor. You haven't wanted to select a sponsor yet, and now you're talking about casting or recruiting someone who hasn't even been born yet! You're asking me to bring my reputation and contacts to bear, and ViralSponsors.com has delivered. So, what are you talking about? Is it a movie, or is it a tournament?"

Halfway through Coco O's rant, he blurted out, "Wade Owen Watts is just a science fiction character. I just happen to know too much trivia." He then swiveled his chair away from her and the whiteboard, starting a conversation with himself, muttering and lightly gesturing with his hands. His face quickly brightened as he pointed his finger in the air.

"We need both a casting call AND a tournament to launch! That's it!" he said proudly. "It'll be loosely based on the Pinocchio character. Buff Pepper will suddenly start talking in a high-pitched voice when he tells a lie. But, he will also be like Gepetto and create a screenplay with Max Pozel as the main character, who we'll bring to life at our press conference - it'll be a 'super duper double looper'! Oh, and Max would also follow the Pinocchio archetype in the sense that when he lies or guesses, he suddenly grows a wagging dog's tail.

It was clear that Lucas was thoroughly satisfied with himself.

Feeling accomplished, like a detective cat solving a mystery involving disappearing yarn balls, Lucas shot out of his chair to walk over to the whiteboard and write BUFF PEPPER in all caps. As he finished, he turned to face Coco, who he was delighted to see was settling back down from her quick bout of frustration over the Max Poz enigma.

"Tell me more about Buff Pepper," she asked.

"Suffice it to say that Buff's uncle was the military guy who founded the Lonely Hearts Club Band," Lucas shot back.

***

Hi there!! Lucas Disney here. Yep, I'm speaking directly to you, the reader (talk about breaking the fourth wall, eh?). Did you think this was going to be a fictional novel? Or perhaps an inspiring non-fiction guide enabling you to bust out and achieve financial independence by maxing out your personal brand? Stick around because it's both, yet neither, and more!

Mark Twain's famous insight is applicable here, "The two most important days of your life are the day you were born and the day you find out why." If you're a goer, your day #2 will happen while you're reading and rereading this tome. As we evolve, our lives are filled with more and more day #2s, which cycle down from a day to just a single moment. Mark Twain was just saying that on a particular day when your life's meaning is revealed, you experience a special moment. So, as you step into who you really are, you begin to experience a few or even a multitude of moments of meaning each day that confirm your *why*.

A good reference point can be found in the lyrics *Tom's Diner* by Suzanne Vega. The singer jumps and bounces in and out of multiple perspectives as she narrates her stream of consciousness while sitting in the diner. While those perspective hops themselves don't deliver on Suzanne Vega's *why*, but her creation of, and performing of, that song does. I suggest you listen to that song and read the lyrics.

In an effort to deliver your *why*, I'll be your navigator on our journey through a sensational tale about XR, a dramatic comedy musical, mock weddings, and fitness competitions hosted by thrivXR (say "thriver").

GUIDING LIGHT MANTRA CHAPTER 2:
I will accept the knowledge that I have a special, unique and irreplaceable gift for humanity.

Chapter Three

The XR Revolution

Enjoy your front seat to the XR Revolution and get ready to experience a bunch of day #2's (i.e. your second most important days, of which you can have many.) Escape Control Central was a whirlwind of innovation and barely contained chaos as Lucas, the mastermind behind thrivXR, laid out his grand vision. Steve, on the verge of escape, had one foot out the door when Lucas's voice thundered through the room.

"WAIT!"

Steve froze, a look of mild panic flashing across his face as he realized his brief moment of freedom was about to be snatched away. Lucas, ever the visionary, was too engrossed in his blueprint for the future to notice Steve's attempted getaway initially.

"Steve, buddy," Lucas began, with a tone that suggested a mix of desperation and inspiration, "could you anchor yourself back into reality for just a smidge longer? There's a brainwave I need to surf with you."

Steve, reluctantly turning back with a sigh that could deflate a balloon, replied, "Alright, but can we fast-track it? Give me the elevator pitch, not the scenic route."

Lucas, undeterred and as enthusiastic as ever, dove headfirst into his spiel. "Picture this: the XR Revolution. We're not just talking about stepping into the future; we're leapfrogging into it. With thrivXR, we're catapulting fitness into the metaverse through our state-of- the-art XR equipment. It's not just exercise; it's an odyssey."

thrivXR equipment profiles.

2024 thrivXR floor layout in uptown Dallas, Texas at 4305 Maple Avenue.

Steve, attempting to keep up, nodded along. "You've mentioned this cosmic journey before, and I'm all in. But remind me, how does this not become a sci-fi fantasy for gym rats?"

"Ah, that's the magic," Lucas beamed, practically vibrating with excitement. "It's our fusion with BeTells. Imagine a synergy so unique that the boutique fitness world will be doing double-takes. We're not just creating a gym but crafting a universe."

Steve, finally catching Lucas's infectious enthusiasm, couldn't help but chuckle. "So, we're essentially building a spaceship with treadmills and calling it innovation?"

Lucas, with a grin as wide as the galaxy they planned to conquer, replied, "Exactly! And with our powers combined, we'll be the captains of this ship. The boutique fitness universe won't know what hit it."

The room, once filled with the imminent threat of a mundane meeting, was now alight with the sparks of creativity and the potential for comedic mishaps. As Lucas and Steve plotted the course for their interstellar fitness odyssey, it was clear that thrivXR was set to be more than just a gym—it would be an adventure.

"So, Lucas..." Steve started off by saying, "you know I'm all in on this and am into leveraging emerging technologies, but I'd like to hear your take on the why and the how of integrating eXtended Reality into a workout."

"Yeah, so here is what I realized," Lucas replies. "I saw that the fitness industry is a bit like the restaurant industry. There's a ton of them, offering mostly the same opportunities, having the same equipment, and always coming and going. It's also a saturated market, so it becomes increasingly challenging to set yourself apart from other gyms. Sure, there are some standouts like Orange Theory, but by and large, most gyms are essentially carbon copies of one another."

"But not thrivXR!" Coco exclaims.

"That's right; not us. No, we are approaching fitness in a way nobody else is. I saw the potential for XR, which is an amalgamation of VR, AI, and AR as well, to enable our members to gamify their workouts in a way that maximizes results and enjoyment. XR provides uniquely immersive workout gaming experiences. Anyone who comes into the thrivXR studio can engage in virtual environments and advanced robotics that make things like running, boxing, and other activities more enjoyable and less monotonous. For example, strengthening core stability is a lot more fun on the Icaros™ flying machine where you are soaring across and around towering mountains."

"It sure is!" shouted out Steve.

"Steve...I have yet to see you on a flying machine," Lucas taunted him.

"Yeah, but I've participated as a spectator, so I basically did, if you think about it that way," Steve said cleverly.

"Ha, yeah, OK, I'll let you have it just so I can keep going with my stream of consciousness," Lucas replied. "XR has the potential to revolutionize the fitness industry by making workouts more engaging, personalized, accessible, and fun! I see the results right here in the studio, where people are approaching physical fitness in a completely new way. A lot of people who have come in here have shared with our staff about how much more they enjoyed their workouts and how the time just flew by, which helped them get a better workout in."

"I am loving everything you're saying right now," chimed in Steve. "It really is a slam dunk to integrate XR into workouts. And it doesn't involve putting on those giant goggles, right?" he asked Lucas.

"Right. XR is all about extending reality, not swapping it out with a virtual one. This means the extensions are usually giant screens on the walls or haptic robots interacting with your physical engagement. It allows for totally immersive training sessions for kickboxing, yoga, cycling, running, and core stability training to maximize results. People really dig our omnidirectional treadmills, flying machines, boxing robots, indoor cycling, and stability clouds."

"Yeah, the boxing robot is one of my favs!" shouted out Steve. "Uh huh..." Coco replied, smirking.

Lucas continued. "So yeah, VR is actually a component of XR, with eyes trained on a screen whose image changes based on the perspective of your visual focus in 3D space. The beauty of XR is that non-VR screens are stationed at focal points where images on those screens respond to your movements. We could go further and say that XR is distinguished from AR and VR with equipment that is impacted, manipulated, and moved by your body and extremities. There are also haptics that provide additional sensory experiences delivered by the virtual gaming environment."

"Sounds kind of like The Matrix, but if everyone wanted to get toned and swole," Coco interjected.

"Bingo!" Lucas replied, "I would say the zeitgeist and perspective of XR is most and best defined by The Matrix trilogy, albeit with an apt and concerning dystopian perspective. In fact, that film series led to a lot of the common concerns with AI, with the most menacing perspective of The Matrix being that AI ends up creating a captive.

and controlling environment to utilize humanity as a power source and computing source."

"Yeah, when you dilute those movies down to that description, it's no wonder people are concerned," added Coco, "even though it's not really like that."

"Right! You and I both know that," Lucas exclaimed. "And that is something similar to what the head of the company that makes the Oculus Quest VR headset said. You see, athletics involves the good of conflict and competition, while war embodies the evil. XR ensures the good of humanity is integrated into AI. There is no putting the genie back in the bottle now, so it's vital to guide and shape AI to mirror the best that humanity has to offer."

Also, today, there are AR games that have both VR and AR capabilities, so when you're putting on a headset, it's no longer necessarily you are blocking out all external real-world input. Special holes in the goggles allow players to see through into the 3D world. I would also add that another zeitgeist-impacting cultural iconic phenomenon is Iron Man, which provides a vision of XR and where it's going."

"I love the Iron Man movies!" shouted our Steve. "Their visual depiction of the direction tech is heading shows us how technological advances can be leveraged in ways that don't seem that far off or out of reach."

"Right," Lucas replied. "And we're showcasing advanced and novel uses of XR tech right here at thrivXR and are at the leading edge of XR possibility!" he explained. It was apparent that the conversation lit a fire of excitement within him.

Lucas kept going. "People who come to thrivXR, which has more XR fitness equipment than any other gym in the world, love the full

freedom of movement the omnidirectional treadmill provides them while being able to walk and run in 360 degrees inside virtual worlds while playing first-person shooters. It's almost like you're not even working out, yet you are getting a better workout than usual! I mean, who wouldn't want to burn calories while kicking zombie and robot ass in an FPS game or dancing to the beat in Rhythm Master while competing with their friends and partners to earn ultimate bragging rights?"

"I'll take you on with the dance machine, but I think I'll stay away from the zombie FPS stuff," Coco informed Lucas.

"I'll be holding you to that," he said with a smile. "That's the beauty of the wide range of machines and XR equipment we have–there's something for everyone."

"So, how does the boxing robot work, exactly?" asked Coco.

"The boxing robot is a really neat addition to the thrivXR studio. It uses AI technology to interpret your movements so that you could get a kick out of fighting zombies with increasing difficulty levels, box to some fresh beats, and transcend high scores," Lucas shared with pride.

"Pretty cool, but I'm more of a cardio girl myself, so remember that I'm beating you on the dance machine," Coco taunted Lucas.

"Since you love cardio, you'll really enjoy our immersive, virtual indoor cycling. It burns fat, improves heart health, and tones muscle, and–," Lucas said before getting cut off by Coco.

"Are you saying I'm fat?" Coco vexed.

"Of course not! I was just–," he started saying before Coco again jumped in.

"I'm just kidding...relax!" she said while laughing.

"You would think after knowing you forever I'd catch onto your brand of humor by now," Lucas said. "So, anyway, the multidimensional training that something like our indoor cycling provides combines cardio exercise with resistance training, and an advanced display system that lets you compare your performance on a leaderboard in real-time."

"Now that's my kind of workout," remarked Coco.

"I think you would also be into the stability clouds," Lucas told her. "They help you improve your core endurance and strength when you participate in virtual ski rides, or while chasing down your prey as a velociraptor. There are many different experiences you could have on the stability clouds...75, in fact!"

"I think the boxing robot is up my alley," commented Steve.

"I see a lot of talk and not a lot of action there, Steve," Lucas quipped. "But since you brought it up, the boxing robot provides on-demand workouts, multiplayer training, animated sparring rounds, total body workouts, and skill assessments that help you track your progress. So, it's a pretty well-rounded XR feature at thrivXR that you really should try out."

"Yeah, yeah, I know. I'll get there sooner or later, but you know my schedule. I'm glad I could stick around to go over the XR integration stuff, but I've got to get going now," Steve told Coco and Lucas.

"Understood. Thanks for doing that. I think we are all on the same page now, which is vital to everything going as smoothly as possible once the rubber meets the road," Lucas replied.

"Totally. Alright, catch you two later," Steve told them.

"Take care, Steve," Coco responded.

"Have a *Max Poz* day, Steve!" Lucas said, smirking to himself at his witty sign-off.

At the heart of the brainstorming session, Lucas, with a flair for the dramatic, marched over to the whiteboard. With the flourish of a seasoned artist, he scrawled two words that seemed to dance with potential:

BUFF PEPPER

He spun around, a conductor ready to gauge the orchestra's reaction, and found Coco, who had just navigated through a sea of frustration, now perched on the edge of her seat with curiosity.

"Buff Pepper?" she echoed, her intrigue piqued.

Lucas's eyes sparkled with the fire of a storyteller about to unveil his magnum opus. "Picture this," he began, "a tale of love, loss, and redemption. Buff Pepper, a divorced dad who missed his shot at love with his high school sweetheart, inadvertently catapults her to stardom. Our saga, Super Duper Double Looper, explores Buff's journey—a whirlwind of creativity and entrepreneurial spirit. His unrequited love fuels his ventures, leading to the birth of a content creation powerhouse. Here, the worlds of celebrity athleticism and XR competitions collide, featuring mock weddings that Buff orchestrates—weddings he never had but can now design for others."

Coco, now thoroughly captivated, sought clarity on the competition's scale. "So, we're launching with a balanced battlefield—64 contenders, split evenly between men and women?"

"Exactly," Lucas confirmed, his nod a seal of commitment to the vision.

"Continue," Coco urged, sensing the story's depth was far from fully explained.

Lucas leaned in as if about to share a secret that could alter the course of entertainment.

"But here's where we transcend the ordinary. As our champions forge alliances, each week blossoms into a spectacle of love and competition. Imagine a new power couple weekly, planning their dream wedding, leading a victory parade, and hosting a grand awards ceremony. This is not just a competition; it's a narrative arc that weaves the adrenaline of athletic prowess with the heart of romantic drama. And then, to elevate the spectacle, they kick off a fresh XR athletic event featuring the zenith of fitness technology—boxing robots, flying machines, omnidirectional treadmills, and avatar racing. It's as if *Back to the Future* crashed into *A Midsummer Night's Dream*, with a detour through *NFL GameDay*, seasoned with the drama of *The Bachelor* and *The Bachelorette*, the innovation of *Shark Tank*, the talent showcase of *The Voice*, and the whimsical storytelling of *Pinocchio*, all trapped in the recurring cycle of *Groundhog Day*."

"That's all? Coco scoffed.

Looking away, Lucas pursed his lips and looked down at his left thumbnail that he had bit this morning when it split because he tried to open his Topo Chico without his bottle opener. Now, tenderly attempting to bite off his hangnail, Lucas turns back to Coco with a lump in his throat born from the fear that this whole vision and all of his planning and investment were a fool's errand.

"Steve, Yolanda…they're on board with this?" Coco asked.

"Yep," replied Lucas dryly, "Don too. Meeting with him later…and amid all of this, Coco Twain develops feelings for Buff, and the two of them awkwardly deal with their emotions for each other as they put together the competition."

"That's awkward; alright. I get it, though. And I see it working," Coco replied cocking her head with a demur but empathetic pout. Coco deeply wanted Lucas to be successful and to win and wondered if his ambitions were insurmountable.

"Of course it will. But now we add the third part of all of this," Lucas said before pausing, "…the *positive* part."

"Okay"? Coco sheepishly responded, wondering what Lucas may dish out next.

"Have you met Don Everyday yet–our General Manager of thrivXR?" Lucas asked her.

"I've seen him, but we haven't been formally introduced," Coco replied.

"Well, today's the day to meet Everyday! He'll be here in a few minutes. Don has broken several world records in javelin and was a star guard in college basketball. He's built, calm, and somewhat stoic; yet everyone knows his presence wherever he goes. He's doing a bang-up job on the club's business launch, so it makes sense to fold him into BeTells Agency and this competition," Lucas informs her.

Lucas went over to his laptop to launch a video call with Don, the GM of thrivXR Fitness Club, who happened to be downstairs at thrivXR. Once the call connected, Don could be seen on the flat-panel TV on the wall.

"Hey, Lucas! The waiting list for members has doubled! What are we going to do?" Don asked.

"Hey, Don! Come up as soon as you can. Coco is here, and we need to chat really quickly about your role in all of this," Lucas told him.

"On my way," Don replied back.

After disconnecting from the video call, Lucas turned toward Coco, seeming to have a brilliant idea. "I've got it! Don will both fictionally function as the GM of thrivXR on the second level of what we're creating here *and* star as Max Pozel on the third level in the Buff Pepper production called *Maximum Positive,* where he creates and promotes the first TriBoxalon," he said. "So, in this *Lucas Disney* production, Max Pozel will become the real Don and will award the winning Buff Pepper and Coco Twain mixed doubles team the $10,000 cash prize. I'd also like to point out that Max Pozel will create a reverse looper on the third level back to Level 2...so the *fictional* Max Pozel will be *both* the real *and* fictional functional Don!"

Coco was truly stunned, saying, "That is truly brilliant!"

Just then, Don walked into Escape Control Central and quietly took a seat by the exit.

"Morning," he told them.

"Great! Now we can start our spiritual practice," Lucas replied quickly in excitement.

"Umm...I thought we were going to talk about the TriBoxalon?" Don asked in confusion.

Lucas stood up and picked up a small mallet on the table, ringing a miniature gong with it that was standing on a small table adjacent to the conference table. He would do this little ritual whenever he felt there was a moment for reflection and contemplation on where things were and where they were headed.

"'The two most important days of your life are the day that you were born and the day you find out why,' ...so says Mark Twain!" Lucas shouted out with conviction before ringing the gong once more. "'The meaning of life is to find your gift. The purpose of life is to give it away,' ...so says Pablo Picasso!" he added to his message to the room.

Before Lucas felt the ritual was complete, he had one more takeaway to give to his small audience, telling them, "...and we conclude with clarity from Maya Angelou, who, in her poetic wisdom, tells us that:

'In the flush of love's light We dare be brave

And suddenly we see That love costs all we are And will ever be.

Yet, it is only love Which sets us free.'"

While looking off into the distance, Lucas told Coco and Don, "This is how I see it...the BeTells service delivery platform will host both an audition in our studio AND an athletic competition thrivXR." Realizing he was in a bit of a trance, he brought his awareness back to the room.

"OK, team," he told them, "one more thing. How about we give our competitors a little freedom? When we give them the script for an audition, we'll tell them they can either *Steer* or *Veer*. *Steer* is where the champions will follow the script we provide them in the audition. If they decide to *Veer*, that's where they'll improvise from the script. What do you think–capeesh?"

"Capeesh," replied Don. "Nothing like shaking things up a little."

So, Don, here's the deal," chimed Coco. "We are launching the first competition, but the Max Pozel character needs to be involved. ViralSponsors.com has the sponsor side of things nailed down."

"That's the best. Great news! I knew ViralSponsors.com would come through," Don told her.

"You know what else is great?" Lucas asked the two while pointing to Don. "*You* are our Max Pozel!"

"Huh?" Don shot back, a bit confused and surprised.

GUIDING LIGHT MANTRA CHAPTER 3:

I love myself with empathy and the knowledge that when I choose to go with the flow, I am doing my very best. Otherwise, I am confident that my intuition will lead me to proactively take decisive action and make meaningful commitments when the time is right.

Chapter Four

The Creed of Champions and the Dominant Brand of Cool

"I am a Champion and you're going to hear me roar."
(from Katy Perry's "Roar")

The dawn of the next morning at thrivXR heralded more than just the arrival of a new day; it marked the beginning of an era with Buff Pepper at its helm. Clad in the latest in athleisure, his physique a testament to the brand's promise, Buff observed the hustle within the gym's walls. His gaze was locked on Max Pozel, an AI android marvel prodigy whose prowess on the gym floor was nothing short of record-breaking. Max, a fixture in the thrivXR landscape, moved with a precision that spoke volumes of his dedication. Each record, he shattered a new benchmark for his peers. Buff, clipboard in hand, surveyed the scene with the focus of a general on the battlefield.

The narrative shifted, transporting Max into a minimalist room yet charged with potential. Here, against the backdrop of a green screen, he stood, paper in hand, his attention oscillating between the document and the formidable duo of Buff Pepper and Coco Twain. Coco, embodying a strength and mystique reminiscent of Coco Oprahprada herself, took her place beside Buff across from Max, their presence a clear signal that the stakes were higher than ever.

"Max, my friend," Buff began, his voice a blend of camaraderie and solemnity. "You stand out as a beacon of talent in this sea of potential. But what unfolds beyond this gym is a saga that demands more than just athletic excellence."

He motioned towards the window, where a line of hopefuls, each embodying the zenith of their discipline, stretched into the distance.

"This line of people, Max, is the embodiment of aspiration and ambition, all vying for a chance to be part of something monumental."

Raising his voice to ensure it carried to every ear in the vicinity, Buff declared, "We are on the brink of launching thrivXR and BeTells into the stratosphere with a competition that is as much about athletic prowess as it is about captivating on-air presence. The victors of this crucible will not only emerge as champions but will also be immortalized in a reality TV series that charts their journey."

Buff's announcement hung in the air, a challenge and an invitation rolled into one. "Our arena welcomes the multifaceted—athletes, artists, influencers—all competing for a spot among the 64 finalists. This is where the realms of acting, professional sports, fitness training, and beyond collide, a battle royale where both male and female Gen-Z luminaries will forge their destinies."

Absorbing the gravity of Buff's proclamation, Max could only muster a simple, "Got it. Cool." Yet, within those words lay an understanding that the path ahead was not just another tournament but a voyage into the very heart of what it means to be a star in the making.

In this charged atmosphere, thrivXR was not just a venue but a launchpad for dreams, where Buff Pepper and Coco Twain were not merely observers but architects of a new reality, ready to redefine the boundaries of athleticism and entertainment.

Back in the real world of thrivXR, Lucas, Don, and Coco O met up at the casting table. The air was thick with anticipation as the trio found themselves on the cusp of merging two worlds—where fiction mirrors reality, and the quest for the next Buff Pepper and Coco Twain was about to unfold.

Lucas, ever the orchestrator of dreams, broke the silence.

"We're standing at the threshold of something monumental, don't you think?" he posed to his comrades. "The casting call for BeTells Champions is not just about filling roles; it's about embodying the spirit of Buff and Coco Twain. We're looking for those who not only resonate with these characters but can also bring them to life."

With a strategic eye, they planned to usher in 64 influencers, each vying for the chance to step into the shoes of the iconic duo.

"The process is rigorous," Lucas outlined. "Not only will they face the camera for their screen tests, but they'll also be put to the test on the thrivXR equipment…their prowess quantified by the TriBoxalon scorecard. And let's not forget the ingenious addition of Yolanda's bracelet-or-chain concept, weaving an extra thread of complexity into the narrative."

Lucas paused, hydrating for the journey ahead, then shared the vision for the next phase with renewed vigor.

"Once the Champions have showcased their mettle, we'll craft a sizzle reel for each contender, a mosaic of their auditions, genuine expressions, and engagements on the Sunglasses With Coco Show. It's not just about finding our stars but discovering the voices that resonate with authenticity."

The room was charged with Lucas's enthusiasm as he unveiled the final twist.

"And then, the power shifts to the audience. Through the democratic lens of online voting, thousands will have their say in determining who will don the mantle of Coco Twain and Buff Pepper. It's an invitation to the masses to shape the narrative."

Despite the whirlwind of planning and strategy, Coco O couldn't help but embrace the humor in Lucas's prediction.

"All the women will want to play me, huh?" she quipped, a light-hearted moment that underscored their camaraderie and shared vision.

This was not just a casting call but a journey into the heart of what makes a character resonate, a blend of competition, innovation, and the collective voice of an engaged audience. As they stood at the crossroads of reality and fiction, Lucas, Don, and Coco O were not just casting for a show…they were curating an experience, a testament to the transformative power of storytelling in the digital age.

Back in the looper, where time bends, and reality twists, Max Poz, Buff, and Coco Twain found themselves at the epicenter of a whirlwind casting day. As the sun dipped below the horizon, casting long shadows over the thrivXR set, Max let out a sigh that seemed to carry the weight of a thousand auditions.

"Whew! It's like we've run a marathon, watched a soap opera, and survived a cooking show finale all in one day. But hey, we've got some serious talent lined up, huh?"

Buff, the ship's captain, nodded, his muscles practically vibrating with anticipation. "Absolutely. Just a sprinkle of strategy here, a dash of planning there, and we'll have the TriBoxalon up and running. I'm so ready, I could bench press a buffalo right now."

As Max vanished into the twilight, eager for whatever rest could be salvaged from such a day, Buff and Coco T were left in the charged silence of the casting room. The air between them crackled, laden with unspoken words and a thick tension that could be sliced with a knife and served on a platter.

Coco T, with a gaze that could only be described as "mystifyingly omniscient," fixed Buff with a look that seemed to peer into the very depths of his soul. Buff, caught in the tractor beam of her stare, felt a familiar dance of electricity zigzagging through the air.

"You just don't get it, do you?" Buff ventured into the void, his voice a blend of exasperation and admiration. "This...thrivXR–it's not just a project. It's my magnum opus...a symphony of sweat and ambition where athletic influencers don't just break a sweat; they break into the spotlight."

But before Buff could further pontificate on his grand vision, Coco Twain interjected with the timing of a seasoned sitcom star, with a drawl dripping with sarcasm.

"Oh, absolutely, Buff... You've got it *all* figured out. It's not like we're trying to juggle flaming torches while riding unicycles here."

The moment hung in the air, a perfect blend of tension and comedic relief as if the universe paused to chuckle at the scene. Here, in this nexus of ambition and aspiration, Buff and Coco T stood as titans of their own making, wrapped in a dance of rivalry and mutual respect, all under the watchful eye of thrivXR's neon green glow.

As the day's chaos settled into the night's calm, the pair realized they were on the brink of something extraordinary despite the jests and jibes. And perhaps, just perhaps, amidst the mock weddings, boxing robots, and avatar racing, there was room for a little love story to unfold in the most unexpected of ways. But that, as they say, is a tale for another day.

Meanwhile, Coco Twain and Buff Pepper sized up the gathering of influencers who waited for their turn to audition for their roles, this time in front of a green screen that projected a scene on a space station. With lightsabers in hand, they went into battle while doing a bit of intense arguing along with it.

"Wait...huh? What's going on here?" Coco Twain asked, completely perplexed by the galactic scene in front of her.

"Oh...I didn't tell you?" Buff replied with a wide grin. "Lucas is working on producing a trilogy called *Planet Peaces* that takes place in a galaxy not-so-far away–far, far in the future with a villain called Light Helmet. He's like if Darth Vader and Dark Helmet had a love child who was obsessed with energy-saving light bulbs...or something. Our hero is a young farm boy with an uncanny ability to navigate bureaucracy to save the galaxy. It's close enough to feel familiar but distant enough to avoid...certain legal entanglements."

There was a long pause, with Coco raising an eyebrow as she was unsure where Buff was going with the idea he was sharing with her.

"Don't you get it?" he said, breaking the silence. "It's a parody of Star Wars and Spaceballs! It stands as a unique beacon of humor and satire within the sci-fi genre."

Coco started taking notes. "Light Helmet, you say? I can already imagine the helmet, part menacing, part ridiculous, with LED lights outlining its features. And I suppose we're aiming for a mix of practical effects and CGI? Spaceballs had its charm with the physical comedy and props.

"Exactly!" Buff exclaimed. "We're going for nostalgia with a modern twist. I want audiences laughing at the absurdity of our special effects yet marveling at their ingenuity."

"What about the plot? Are we thinking of episodic adventures, or is there a larger narrative at play?"

"A little bit of both. Each film in the trilogy will have its own arc, but there'll be a thread connecting them—our heroes' quest to bring peace to the galaxy by assembling an ancient artifact, the Peacekeeper before Light Helmet does.

"I could see that working. We can play with so many sci-fi tropes while telling a compelling story. The balance of parody and homage is key."

"Exactly what I was thinking. We're not just making fun of the genre but showing our love for it. And with *Planet Peaces*, we'll create something that fans of those iconic films can enjoy while drawing in a new audience."

After initial skepticism, their vibe shifted to one of agreement and shared excitement for the novel production concept.

"Of course, Lucas throws us into the deep end here with his imagination." she said back, realizing it was all starting to make sense.

"Yep. You know how he is. He's a wickedly creative guy, though, you have to admit." Buff told her, looking to get her validation.

"I do," she chimed back before quickly changing the subject. "Look, kid. Hey, I know you're an affable guy and all that, and I'm only a year older than you, and we've been friends for a long time..." Coco Twain took a dramatic breath before continuing, "...and your folks believed in me enough to get me on the road to where I wanted to go...but they're small time. I had to move on, and it was a good

business decision, you have to admit. Look, nobody deserves what I have. I am lucky, but let me tell you something–I bust my ass..."

Buff abruptly cut her off in mid-sentence, saying, "Let me tell you something. I know all about you, where you come from, and you work hard..."

Before Buff could get another word in, Coco bulldozed his train of thought. "*Work hard?* What in the world do you know about my art– my creative process and what I need to do to succeed? I am an artist. What do *you* know about creating a masterpiece?"

Buff stood silent and dumbfounded, with his eyes widened to their limits as he stared at Coco T. Being met with his reaction made her go silent for a moment, but she then continued her diatribe with increasing intensity until it built into a fiery fury.

"Every masterpiece is delivered by a muse on loan from an angel. What do you know about my art? What makes you think you can be the best talent agent on the planet? That's what I wanna know because that's what I deserve. Why do you deserve to be the CEO of the BeTells Creative Reality TV Agency? Sure, both your parents are talent agents; but why in the world would I EVER trust you with my career?" she fired at him.

Buff took a moment to let everything she said sink in before sitting up straighter and taller as he looked off into the imaginary beyond. He began his rebuttal, which sounded quite indignant, poetic, and Shakespearean in its gravitas.

"I have a giant standing on my shoulder...whispering in my ear...a muse for all seasons. With luck, he surrenders to angelic sparks to channel silent vibrations. So, I must relent, irrevocably yielding to my active imagination to drown reality and yield to an undulating sensation."

Buff paused before continuing.

"With a deafening silence, my muse welcomes hospitality on my shoulder, driving me to be bolder than the fear of the blank page. The attention of the universe bears down on me...and in awe, I become a vessel with my naked body and perfect mind on stage. Today's dynamic is pounding out the vibe from Andy Warhol that life is art, and art is business...and that's OK. In a perfect world, theory and practice are two sides of the same coin, but they are different...and that is especially true in the reality TV business. Most essentially, you're not living until you're giving."

Buff's words were clearly stunning Coco. However, he wasn't quite finished just yet. Buff took a big inhale before moving on.

"Here's why I want to be the guy behind the guy behind the guy: I have so much to share, but I know there is no fairness. So, I stand, deliver, take the blame, and know I'm flawed before my God. I wear my sin and glow in the dark, ashamed of my stark-naked mark...and then I remember: the real mark I make is yet to take hold, grow, deliver, and bestow. So, here I go, avoiding the heat of the flame of fame, which is my process to create a massive gift of love drowning hate. Shredding risk and recycling my experience, I hope to make a dramatic difference. So, as you go, please know that your words have meaning and may stain my name...but at least I gave my all."

Buff finally came back down to reality and stared plainly at Coco Twain. "Thanks for listening and witnessing my soul bleeding."

Coco returned his stare with a blank state of her own. She was definitely not expecting what she just saw and heard.

"Buff, you're a very passionate creative. You're a successful guy, and you've done right by me," Coco told him before she paused, her countenance suddenly changing to flirtatious. Buff's eyes became as wide as saucers as he wondered in shock as to what was happening. Coco continued, telling him, "All these years and you've never had a crush on me?" At this point, Buff was an absolute deer in headlights. Coco listened and waited for his response to what she had just laid out before him.

"Uuhhhhh...rrrrright....abjfagbaj. I have not..." Buff had been completely blindsided by what Coco had just expressed to him. Suddenly, he winced and groaned in pain and agony as Coco reached under the table they were sitting at now looking gazing eye to eye as she gently caressed his thigh slowly working up to a gentle yet firm grip on Buff.

"This doesn't let you lie now, does it?" Coco remarked with a heavy breath and light chuckle soaking up Buff's gaze.

"No, not really," Buff managed to eke out.

At this point, Coco had placed all her cards on the table (figuratively), and it became clear to them that their passion for one another was indeed mutually met. After Coco T sang a provocatively personal song describing her desire for all manner of sensuality and parenthood involving Buff, he frantically looked around the table, quickly shuffling around his papers and pen until he finally found what he was looking for: a humble paperclip. He fashioned this wiry nic nac into a ring before placing it on Coco's outstretched finger...

It wasn't long before the day of their opulent outdoor wedding came–a dream come true for the two of them. As they faced one another dressed to the matrimonial nines, they smiled as a minister held a Bible and nodded to the couple. It was finally happening.

Back in the Escape Control Central, Lucas, Coco O, Yolanda, Y-Ali, Steve, and Don were all seated around the conference table. Y-Ali was the first to say something.

"Wow...OK, wait, I have a question, "Y-Ali interjected quickly. "So, about the competitions, can you explain a little bit more about those and how they relate to the scene with Coco T and Buff?"

"Can do," Lucas replied. "The plan is to have upcoming regularly occurring thrivXR competitions that include the unique twist of our Champions auditioning for a dramatic comedy role. As part of the roles they will play, we will also include weekly recurring mock weddings. And we're also going to have charities involved so that there is a giving element to it all. So, this is a completely unique and one-of-a-kind endeavor we are embarking on together here. Buff Pepper is a divorced father who didn't marry his high school crush but is responsible for her rise to fame. As for Buff, he's a creative and successful entrepreneur who channels his explosive passion for the inaccessible love of his life into his work. His creative struggles result in sensational businesses that are the product of his content creation studio that monetizes creative and athletic celebrities with regular eXtended Reality, or XR, with competitions that include weekly recurring mock weddings. Buff Pepper is also the one who produces the Maximum Positive production, which he creates and promotes the first TriBoxalon."

"That's cool," Y-Ali said back. "So, I get the whole Coco Twain and Buff level, but where's Max again? Is that on the same level or another one down?"

"That's one more level out from Coco T and Buff," Lucas clarified. "Max Pozel is a really amazing character because he is the token fitness influencer. Basically, if you looked up 'Fitness Influencer' in the dictionary, you would probably see him mentioned as THE example. But I like your question, so I will unpack a little more about a model fitness influencer. But hey, we could also say here that the dictionary would have Don's name there," he said while everyone in the room laughed. "But yeah, Max is the ultimate competitor at thrivXR. He breaks all the records on the machines, has the voice of a Grammy-winning artist, drives a flashy car, and all of it. You could say he's the total package."

"Sure sounds like my kind of man," Y-Ali remarked as she smirked.

"And like I was saying," Lucas continued, "The kind of people we are looking for to become Champions are those men and women who are entrepreneurial-minded fitness influencers, former and existing pro athletes, aspiring movie and TV stars, and people who want to grow and monetize their herd. We want the go-getters who are looking to achieve wealth through self-actualization."

"Well, talk is talk, and I'll believe it when I see it, " Y-Ali interrupted, forever the contrarian with no filter deadpans.

Coco winced at Y-Ali's remark. "Let me tell you something, sister- girl. You're probably the type of clairvoyant who can see a trend before it happens. Aren't you?"

Y-Ali, smiling, stood up, nodding as her hand moved to her hip.

"So, you probably drive by a corner and say that would be a great location for a 7-11 and then take pride when you see one get put in a year or two later," continued Coco with a charming smile.

Y-Ali, still nodding with a growing smile, cocked her head back, feeling more relaxed at the acknowledgment.

"Well!" Coco started saying in a firm tone, eyes tightened to a laser beam staring at Y-Ali ratatats. "Lucas sees a corner like that, puts it under contract for 1% earnest money, holds it for 13 months, gets it entitled at the city, signs a lease with corporate 7-11 AAA credit rating at more than double the price/sf, rental than the prior tenant for 75% of the interior space, on an 'as is' basis, and requires 7-11 to pump one million bucks into improving the property and arranges 125% loan to cost of the project, and walks away from the closing table with $50,000 in cash and 100% ownership of an asset that throws off $250,000 annually after debt service." She paused for dramatic effect.

"Lucas is money," Coco whispered.

Y-Ali's eyes popped, and she sat down. "I get it. OK. Wow....cool...."

"Great!" Lucas said after standing up and clapping his hands once. "Now we can really get started. Let's get straight to work and continue our planning for the launch of BeTells–a talent agency for professional gaming athletes and artists to grow their fanbase and monetize their herd. Our first order of business..." Lucas was cut off by Steve wanting to interject something that was clearly on his mind.

"Excuse me," Steve started saying, "...as part of launching this agency, and as a founding investor and branding expert, it's vital that I go through my branding process to create the brand. With that, we must understand Project Allegory so that we can launch the Dominant Brand of Cool." Steve could see he now had a confused yet attentive audience.

"Project Allegory?" Yolanda asked him.

"Exactly!" It's actually a historical analysis of the Dominant Brand of Cool that starts with Eve biting the Apple in the Garden of Eden." To help illustrate what he was trying to articulate, Steve picked up a marker and drew a timeline on the whiteboard in the room, explaining each shape and arrow as he continued.

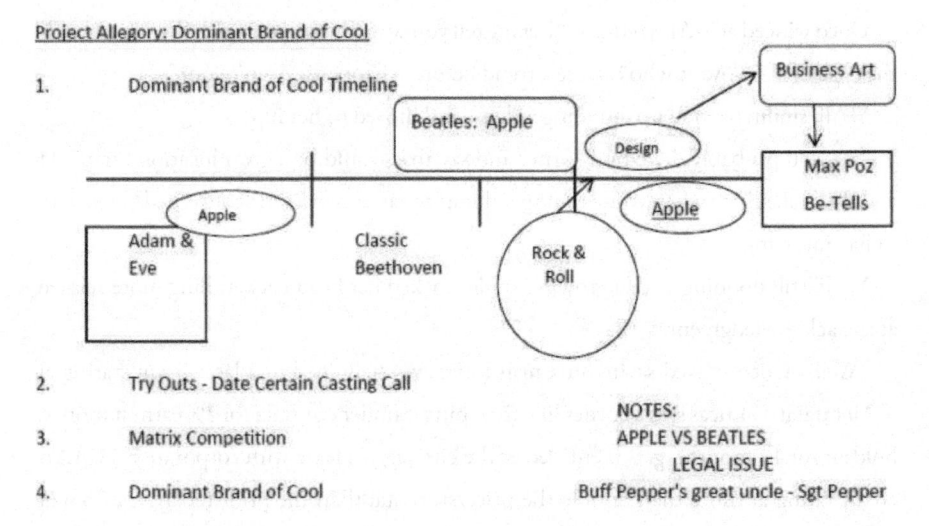

Project Allegory: Dominant Brand of Cool

1. Dominant Brand of Cool Timeline

   - Adam & Eve (Apple)
   - Classic Beethoven
   - Beatles: Apple
   - Design
   - Rock & Roll (Apple)
   - Business Art
   - Max Poz Be-Tells

2. Try Outs - Date Certain Casting Call
3. Matrix Competition
4. Dominant Brand of Cool

NOTES:
APPLE VS BEATLES
LEGAL ISSUE
Buff Pepper's great uncle - Sgt Pepper

"Now, I've already bounced this off of Lucas here, but it all starts with Adam and Eve, see?" he said, pointing to the whiteboard. "They ate the apple, and while, unfortunately, things went a little south for them, it's all about independence from authority. Fast-forward, and we've got Beethoven's genius setting the ultimate bar for talent outside of the church. Then, look what happens–rock and roll explodes on the scene. Then, here come The Beatles. What's their record label? Ah! It's Apple! Apple Records and The Beatles: lucrative, business-savvy, and brilliant with their talent. So, this timeline tracks the Dominant Brand of Cool. Historically and mythologically, The Beatles and Apple are linked..." Steve looked over his drawn diagram on the whiteboard with satisfaction, briskly tossing his marker onto the conference table before sitting down.

"I'm trying to think back to a time when I saw something nerdier than this," Coco said before intentionally pausing for a moment. "Nope. Can't think of it."

Yolanda decided to chime in, asking Steve, "Where is the heart in this, anyway, Steve?"

"You lost me at 'The Beatles.' They didn't use autotune back then, did they? If they did, then that is SO not right!" Y-Ali added.

Don, who also was ready to jump on the bandwagon to dismiss Steve, asked Lucas a blunt question. "So, Lucas, what's the plan?"

Lucas had sensed that Steve had definitely lost everyone. He tried to get the focus back on substance in a show of solidarity. "What are you even talking about? Nobody cares about how you came up with the name. We just want to know what it is..."

"Yes," Steve replied. "We'll get back to that. So...Project–"

Seeing how Steve seemed to continue acting deaf, Lucas became quite infuriated. "What is the name? Just tell us, PLEASE!" he pleaded.

Realizing he had the start of an angry mob on his hands, Steve made a few clicks with his mouse until the BeTells Creed appeared on the flatscreen on the wall. Everyone read what appeared in front of them. It was a foundational code of guidance for the BeTells Creative Reality TV Agency.

BE (a champion) TELL (the world)

CHAMPION CREED:

Athleticism reveals my truth. Charity delivers my promise.

Competition reconciles my humanity. CHAMPION REALITY:

When you wish to be a star,

You're just like those who already are. Live your creed to create your legend. Participate and Impact Now.

BE   **TELL**
a champion   the world

CHAMPION CREED:
Athleticism reveals my truth.
Charity delivers my promise.
Competition reconciles my humanity.

CHAMPION REALITY:
When you wish to be a star,
    you're just like those who already are.
Live your creed to create your legend.
Participate and Impact Now.

BE A CHAMPION!

Be Tells
Creative Reality TV Agency

I can get behind that," Y-Ali remarked as the rest of the room nodded in agreement.

"Glad to hear it!" Steve exclaimed in excitement. He was worried that it was touch-and-go for a bit but was finally relieved. If only he were as good at explaining things as he was with all of the tech stuff he was a savant in.

"This is *everything*," Coco remarked. "Steve, you came up with this?" she asked.

"The Creed? he asked rhetorically. "No, that's Lucas' brainchild.

The Champion Creed won Coco's heart and mind and captured her imagination from a professional standpoint, given that she was a brilliant genius. Given her natural talents and abilities, she was propelled into the stardom she acquired at a very early age. She was a child prodigy and was a respected concert pianist at the young age of five. Later on, she developed an AI tool that decoded 30% of the human genome. That accomplishment is, in fact, what drew Steve into her orbit.

But, as brilliant as she was, Coco was also in extreme awe of Lucas' creative genius. This made her feel a bit vulnerable when it came to her feelings for him. She was no stranger to achievement. Her life was a tapestry of success, woven from her talents and intellect. However, as she sat there, enveloped by Lucas' created world, she could not shake off a tinge of feeling inadequate–a feeling that gnawed at her from the inside.

Lucas had always inspired her with his relentless creativity and ability to bring the most fantastical ideas to life. Yet, lately, this inspiration was overshadowed by a sense of vulnerability. Coco admired Lucas not just for his professional achievements but for the person he was—passionate, dedicated, and endlessly inventive. Their long-standing friendship had been a source of comfort and joy, but Coco had always harbored deeper feelings for Lucas...feelings she had kept (or at least tried to) hidden beneath layers of camaraderie and professional respect. However, in recent times, this was becoming harder and harder.

The very thought of revealing her true heartfelt feelings filled her with a sense of dread because to do so would expose her to potential rejection. This was a risk that threatened to shatter the carefully maintained equilibrium of their relationship. Her admiration for Lucas's genius was a two-edged sword. On one hand, it drew her closer to him, yet on the other, it amplified her insecurities. Her feelings haunted her, casting a shadow over her achievements and leaving her feeling exposed and uncertain. The thought of confessing her feelings to Lucas was fraught with the potential for heartache, yet concealing her true emotions felt increasingly untenable.

Coco stood at a crossroads. The realization that her feelings might remain unreciprocated was a bitter pill to swallow, yet the prospect of never exploring the depths of their connection was equally unbearable. She was jostled out of a deeply reflective state by Steve moving on with his presentation.

"Now that I've wet your whistle with that, I'd like to share a little bit about Project Bean."

"Great, another Project," Coco said as she rolled her eyes.

"Very funny, Coco, but I think you'll like it, as will the rest of you," Steve shot back.

Steve switched over to another presentation that he displayed on the screen for everyone to see. PROJECT BEAN in giant, all-capital letters was emblazoned across the display, with "It's a Magic Bean" placed as a tagline underneath it.

It's a new way of life.
Project Bean is about a magic bean.
But it is just a project name, and there is no bean.

Steve's presentation showed off a new scheduling style for team members that maximized reliability, training, pay, and produced the best team possible. What he was presenting was a new way of life for the team, which started with initial training that ensured everyone started off on the right foot. The presentation explained how to "harvest the bean" and extract the maximum value while delivering just as much back.

It's a new way of life

Project Bean is about a magic bean and a magic carrot. But there is no bean

But there is a carrot.

[Slide: PROJECT BEAN — It's a magic bean / thrivXR]

[Slide: ABOUT THE BEAN — It's a new way of life. Project Bean is about a magic bean. But it is just a project name and there is no bean. / thrivXR SPORTS + FITNESS]

CODE OF BOUNTY COPY 67

OPTION

7 DAYS ON 7 DAYS OFF

Schedules begin on Wednesday and end on Tuesday.

2 WEEKS OF PAY EVERY PERIOD

BeTells Champions receive a full paycheck every pay period.

7 DAYS ON 7 DAYS OFF / 2 FREE WEEKENDS EVERY 4 WEEKS / 2 FULL PAYCHECKS

MONDAY	TUESDAY	WEDNESDAY	THURSDAY	FRIDAY	SATURDAY	SUNDAY
1 OFF	2 OFF	3 ON	4 ON	5 ON	6 ON	7 ON
8 ON	9 ON	10 OFF	11 OFF	12 OFF ☀	13 OFF	14 OFF
15 OFF	16 OFF	17 ON	18 ON	19 ON	20 ON	21 ON
22 ON	23 ON	24 OFF	25 OFF	26 OFF ☀	27 OFF	28 OFF

☀ = PAYDAY

PROJECT BEAN

OPTIONAL SCHEDULE

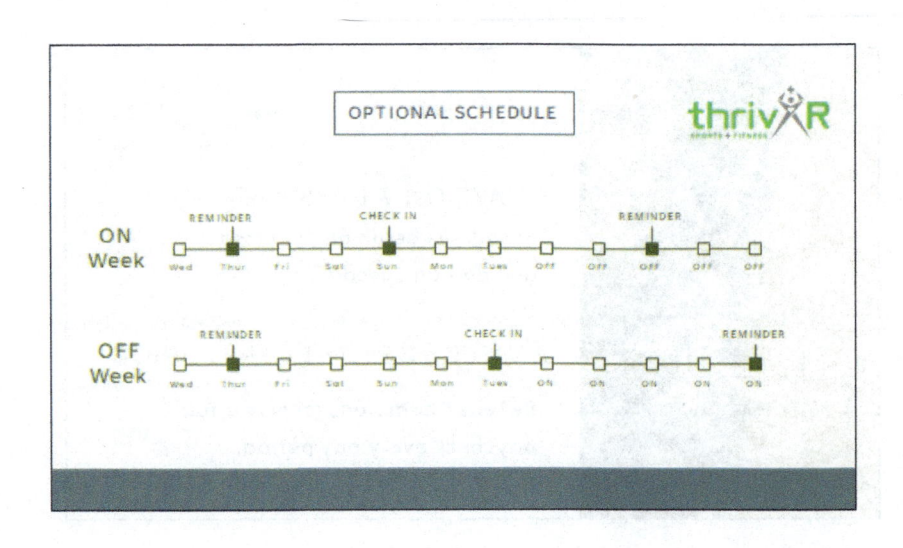

		REMINDER			CHECK IN				REMINDER			
ON Week	Wed	Thur	Fri	Sat	Sun	Mon	Tues	Off	Off	Off	Off

		REMINDER				CHECK IN					REMINDER
OFF Week	Wed	Thur	Fri	Sat	Sun	Mon	Tues	On	On	On	On

LIFE SCHEDULE SIMPLIFIED

Does running late count as exercise?

CODE OF BOUNTY COPY 69

PROJECT BEAN IS...
...AN OPTION

- [x] OPTIONAL
- [x] 12 HOUR SHIFTS
- [x] MORE PAY

thrivXR

HARVEST BEST SHIFTS

Project Bean is a new way of life.

> **Flexibility.**
>
> **Simplicity.**
>
> **Maximize life fulfillment.**

BENEFITS

PROJECT BEAN

It's a new way of life.

Project Bean is a magic bean & a magic carrot.

But there is no bean.
But there is a carrot.

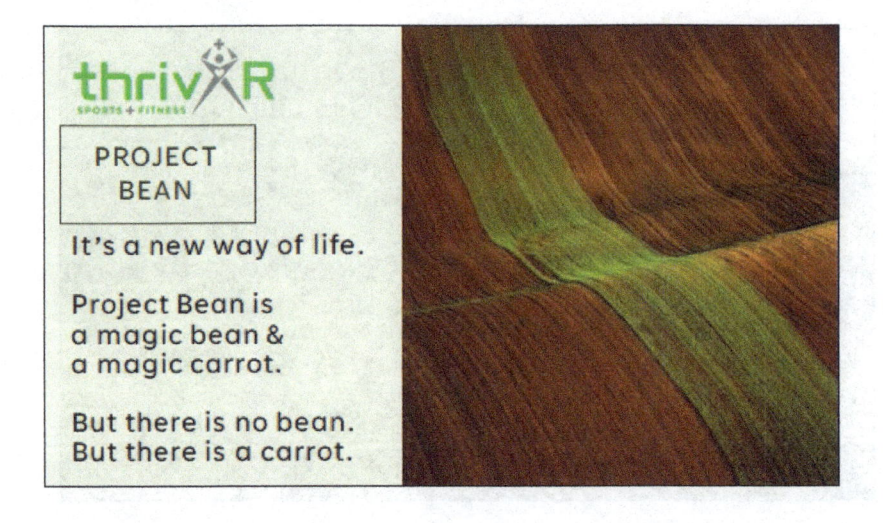

"Alright, now I'm done," Steve told everyone. He knew he was risking the pitchforks after doing two back-to-back presentations, but thankfully, the crowd had settled.

Lucas stood up, getting ready to call the meeting to an end. "Thanks, Steve. I think those presentations helped everyone here understand what we're fixing up to do here a little bit more."

"And I'm sure we'll have to elaborate more at the next meeting!" Steve said while chuckling to himself.

"We're all looking forward to it," Coco said with a smirk.

<u>GUIDING LIGHT MANTRA CHAPTER 4:</u>

The reason that there is no magic bean is because I am the magic.

Chapter Five

Transformational Leadership through Service Excellence

As the meeting edged towards its conclusion, the air in the room, thick with anticipation of dismissal, was suddenly charged with Lucas's earnest declaration.

"Before we dash off to conquer our respective worlds, there's a vital beacon I need to shine on something close to my heart," Lucas announced, his voice a blend of solemnity and fervor. "It's about elevating our pursuit of Service Excellence to forge not just leaders, but Transformational Leaders."

Coco, ever the embodiment of patience stretched thin, gave Lucas a weary glance. "Dive into your passion, Lucas," she said, her tone laced with a hint of resignation yet flavored with respect for his passion. "But let's not forget, my calendar isn't a luxury—it's a battlefield."

Lucas launched into his presentation undeterred by Coco's veiled warning and with the promise of being brief. The room's focus shifted to the glowing screen where thrivXR's Mission, Values, and Vision unfurled like a flag of great purpose.

"Service Excellence," Lucas began, his voice carrying the weight of the concept, "isn't just a pair of words to us...it's the very soil from which we aim to cultivate a forest of Transformational Leaders—our Champions, our team, and our cherished clients."

With a strategic pause, Lucas advanced to a slide that seemed to hold the essence of thrivXR itself—the Core Values. Now enraptured in his narrative, the room watched as these values were not merely presented but woven into a tapestry of ambition and intent.

CORE VALUES

- Attract

- Gather

- Play

- Evolve

- Thrive

Pointing to the screen with a pen that suddenly seemed more like a wand, Lucas conjured visions of a future underpinned by these values.

"These pillars," he articulated with the precision of a poet, "are the compass by which we navigate our quest for transformative leadership." One by one, Lucas dove into each core value, his words painting a vivid picture of a community where attracting like-minded souls, gathering them into a nurturing fold, engaging in the playful yet profound act of growth, evolving beyond the confines of yesterday, and thriving in the fullness of their potential, were not just aspirations but inevitable outcomes.

Initially brimming with the restlessness of impending departure, the room was now in full attention, captivated by the vision Lucas laid before them. Even Coco, who had been poised on the brink of impatience, found herself drawn into the gravitational pull of Lucas's vision, her earlier skepticism slowly melting away under the warmth of his convictions.

thrivXR Business Plan

100% COMMITTED to LONG TERM VISION with daily focus on POSITIVE RESULTS through SERVICE EXCELLENCE.

thrivXR
thrivXR is an equal opportunity employer

thrivXR VALUES

1. Attract
Emanate energizing healthy magnetic vibes and utilize gravity and inertia to ignite sensational positive change and personal growth.

2. Gather
Welcome champions, members and guests to engage together in self evolving legend creation.

3. Play
Have fun!

4. Evolve
Let your life experience nourish your soul.

5. Thrive
Quench Your Best Self!

thrivXR
thrivXR is an equal opportunity employer

CODE OF BOUNTY COPY

thrivXR PURPOSE

VALUES:
- Attract
- Gather
- Play
- Evolve
- Thrive

Our purpose is to provide soul nourishment to maximize talent + help others thrive.

thrivXR VISION:

Create the most compelling sports + fitness company of the 21st century by leading the world's shift to gamify sports + fitness with XR.

thrivXR MISSION

To revolutionize the sports + fitness world by gamifying sports + fitness with XR.

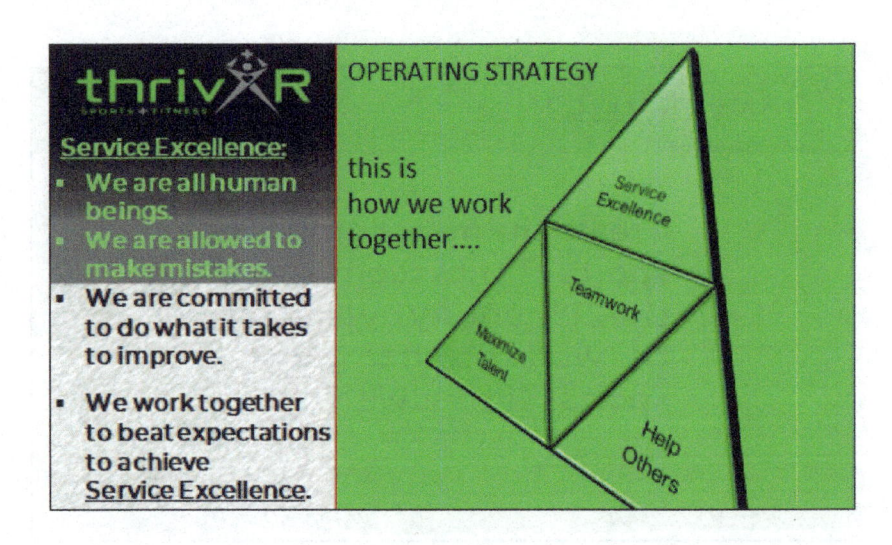

thrivXR

OPERATING STRATEGY

thrivXR

Service Excellence:
- We are all human beings.
- We are allowed to make mistakes.
- We are committed to do what it takes to improve.
- We work together to beat expectations to achieve **Service Excellence**.

this is how we work together....

- Service Excellence
- Teamwork
- Maximize Talent
- Help Others

thrivXR Company Culture

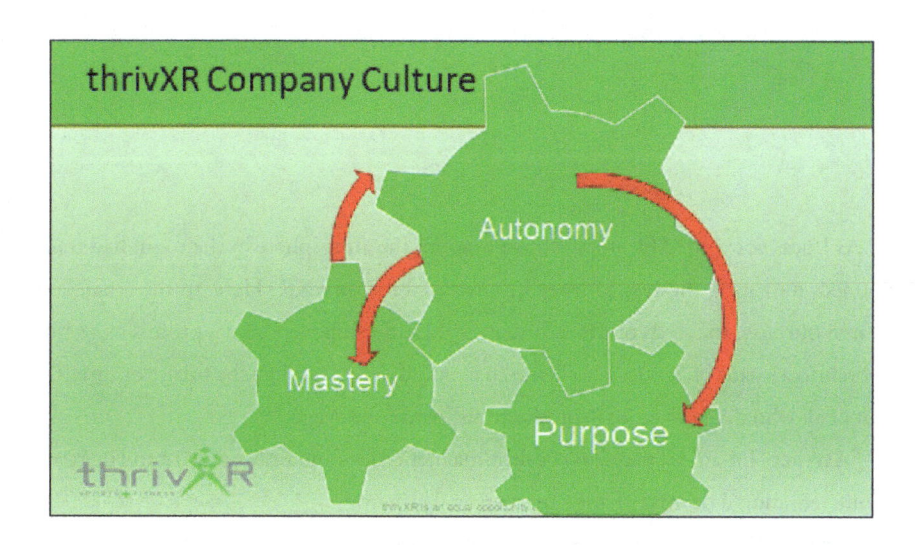

- Autonomy
- Mastery
- Purpose

Emotional Intelligence

Honesty – the commitment and skill to be honest with our selves and others.

- Self-awareness – the ability to recognize and understand your moods, emotions and drives as well as their effect on others.

- Self-regulation – the ability to control or redirect your impulses especially when they are negative or disruptive. The ability to think before you act and to maintain professionalism at all times.

- Motivation – a passion to work for reasons that go beyond money or status.

- Empathy – the ability to understand where other people are coming from. Compassion for self.

- Social Skill – the proficiency to build relationships and influence others.

As Lucas concluded his impassioned oration, the atmosphere in the room had transformed, mirroring the very journey he envisaged for thrivXR. Here, in the crucible of shared purpose, the seeds of Transformational Leadership were sown, promising to burgeon into a legacy of Service Excellence that would define not just the future of thrivXR, but of all who dared to embark on this transformative voyage.

"**Attract**–Emanate energizing healthy magnetic vibes and utilize gravity and inertia to ignite sensational positive change and personal growth.

Gather–Welcome Champions, members, and guests to engage in self-evolving legend creation.

Play–Have fun!

Evolve–Let your life experience nourish your soul.

Thrive–Quench Your Best Self!"

Lucas looked around the room to make sure everyone was fully absorbing the gravitas of what he was sharing.

"Since everyone in this room is a key member of the endeavor we are embarking on here, you should already be familiar with our stated Purpose, which is to maximize talent and help others with XR."

"Right on!" Steve shouted out, noticeably beaming with the mention of XR. "I think XR is one of the current emerging technologies being underutilized at the moment, which is a big reason why I was so gung-ho about being a part of thrivXR. I see the absolutely massive potential for XR helping others, so it was an easy decision for me," he added.

"I'm glad you said that, Steve," Lucas replied. "And as far as maximizing talent goes, we help guide people towards their strengths and passions, provide education and training, as well as monitoring and supervision, and also conduct research and assessment."

Pausing as if thinking of how to formulate his next words, Lucas figured out what to say.

"Service Excellence is a bit of an operating system. Overall, we should always strive to exceed expectations. We should be proactive and responsive, show compassion, follow outlined processes and procedures, and radiate positivity."

"Did somebody say processes and procedures?" Coco chimed in. She was a sucker for standard operating procedures and was really concerned with making sure they were followed. "I had a few thoughts about SOPs for thrivXR and BeTells, actually. What I believe would improve the efficiency of our team and tie into providing service excellence is that everyone would take standard working hours to ensure healthy work-life balance and be a part of the de facto community we are creating."

"I'm listening," Lucas said.

"So, how about release dates for when appointments will be available, which will become special announcements that will occur based on what's going on? Also, what if we have a waitlist people can sign up for, and once it's full, a release date will come out at that point? I also think that all competitions and classes should be available to see when the tipping points start to happen. People will be able to bring in friends at a group rate," Coco explained with excitement.

"All great ideas, Coco," Lucas replied. "I assume this is more focusing on BeTells, right?" he asked her.

"Yes, what I'm concentrating on here is prospective class leaders. These would be people initially getting trained by BeTells, and the interviews will largely happen on video. Basically, an online training course of sorts that has been expertly crafted to help achieve that excellence we are after," she said. "Oh, and the SOP would be a living document because things happen when they happen, as you know, Lucas," Coco added.

"I sure do," he said. "And coming back to Service Excellence, there are five key points I would like everyone in this room to commit to memory.

We are all human beings.

We are allowed to make mistakes.

We are committed to doing what it takes to improve.

We set expectations that our operational systems will beat.

We work together to beat expectations to achieve Service Excellence.

Lucas paused for a moment to make sure the gang was absorbing these essential components of his concept of transformational leadership through service excellence. He then continued, expanding on each point.

"We are all human beings–obvious enough, but what does this mean in terms of Service Excellence?" he asked rhetorically. "What this emphasizes is the importance of empathy and understanding. As humans, we can recognize that everyone, be they a staff member, client, or stakeholder, is a human being with unique needs, feelings, and challenges. By cultivating a culture of respect, kindness, and consideration, we ensure an inclusive environment where everyone feels valued and heard. It's essentially a human-centric approach that follows the Golden Rule," he said before taking a moment and continuing on.

"We are allowed to make mistakes–even Champions can goof up! To err is human, and this principle champions a growth mindset. We understand that mistakes are vital to learning and becoming a master of our craft. We foster a culture of creativity and neverending improvement by encouraging our team and Champions to take calculated risks and experiment with creative reality. When mistakes happen, we focus on learning from them instead of blaming someone. This approach helps accelerate personal and professional growth and propels thrivXR towards novel ideas and solutions...as it already has!" Lucas was proud of himself, given that everyone in the room nodded their heads in agreement at this being reflected within the thrivXR Fitness Studio and not just an empty platitude.

He continued.

"We are committed to doing what it takes to improve—and don't we know it! This value speaks to our dedication to service excellence in a big way. We aren't satisfied with the status quo, as that creates complacency, and things start falling by the wayside. Instead, we constantly look for ways to enhance our services and processes. This commitment involves actively requesting feedback, investing in improving our staff and Champions, and staying up-to-date on the latest innovations and improvements in XR. Basically, it's all about proactively identifying where improvement can take place, and always working to implement effective solutions."

"That's what I always remembered about you, Lucas," Coco interjected. "You were always a go-getter who strived to be the best you could be at something."

"And so were you!" he exclaimed as the two shared a knowing glance that transmitted nostalgic memories they both had.

"Speaking of being go-getters, our fourth key point for Service Excellence is that we set expectations that our operational systems will beat. This value reflects our great ambitions and high standards. We designed our operating systems so that they not only meet expectations but exceed them. To do this, we set challenging yet attainable goals, monitor performance closely, and stay agile enough to make any necessary adjustments. When we keep raising the bar, we make sure thrivXR isn't just keeping up with competitors, but actually leading the way in the boutique fitness industry." Lucas took a breath and a moment before expanding on his last point.

"We work together to beat expectations to achieve Service Excellence. This one underscores just how important teamwork and collaboration are in achieving our goals. There's no 'I' in 'team', and teamwork makes the dream work!" Lucas said, amused at himself for his corniness.

"Good one, Lucas," Y-Ali retorted.

"Anyway," he went on, "we understand that Service Excellence isn't something we can achieve in isolation. It requires the collective efforts of everyone to complete lots of 'todo's.' on our team because each team member brings their unique skills, experience, and perspectives to the table. When create innovative solutions and deliver exceptional service that sets us apart from our competitors."

Lucas sat down after his presentation had finally come to a close, with the room both noticeably receptive and squirmy by now.

"I know I've kept you all here for quite some time, and I see some here are itching to go to the bathroom, so I will close this out by saying that each of these values is integral to the thrivXR ethos. They are here to help guide our decisions, shape our culture, and drive us toward actualizing our mission. I think if we all remember these, we can excel in our commitment to Service Excellence," Lucas told them.

"And also our mission statement!" Coco shouted out.

"That's right. *'To revolutionize the sports and fitness world by gamifying sports and fitness with XR.'*" Lucas added. "I believe we have what it takes to actualize our mission to create the most compelling sports and fitness company of the 21st century by leading the world's shift to gamify sports and fitness with XR."

"And our purpose is to provide soul nourishment to maximize talent and help others with XR," added Steve.

"Exactly! Glad you remembered that one, Steve," Lucas exclaimed with glee. "I always strive to take someone exactly where they want to go with their career because that is what I believe a truly transformational leader does. The best leaders show others how to be leaders of their lives," he added.

"And that's why we love you," Coco commented.

"You're too kind, but thanks," he responded, slightly blushing.

"Alright, I think we can stop it there. Thanks, everyone, for coming today. I'll catch you on the flip," Lucas told the room.

"Actually, not!" Steve shouted out, stone-cold and curt. All eyes were suddenly on Steve.

"All thrivXR staff will assume the persona of one of the BeTells and stay in character. So, the standard operational procedure for the operation of thrivXR will take on the ethic Disney instilled in his theme parks, where each staff member remains in character. "Lucas shouted out, "That's sensational!

GUIDING LIGHT MANTRA CHAPTER 5:
Unleashing my inner light will bring the bounty of the world to my door.

Chapter Six

Champions of thrivXR

The dawn of a new day at thrivXR brought the promise of progress as the core team assembled for a pivotal huddle in Escape Control Central. Lucas, Coco, and Steve were the brains behind the operation, each bringing their unique flair to the table. The air was charged with anticipation as they prepared to delve deeper into the essence of what makes thrivXR tick: the Champions.

"Appreciate you all making the time. Today's discussion is crucial, so I encourage jotting down any lightbulb moments," Lucas initiated.

Coco, with a confidence that bordered on legendary, flashed a cheeky grin. "Note-taking? Please, my brain snaps pictures better than a high-end DSLR."

Steve, momentarily caught off guard by Coco's audacious claim, teetered on the brink of a technical rebuttal. "I'm not quite sure that's how a photogra..." He caught himself mid-sentence, wisdom prevailing over the urge to correct her. Coco had a knack for verbal judo, turning even the most well-intentioned comments into comedic comeuppance.

Refocusing the discussion, Lucas dove into the heart of the matter.

"To kick things off, let's clarify our understanding of what it means to be a Champion. It's not just a title; it's a commitment. A Champion is someone who stands in the arena for something greater than themselves, be it a competition or a cause."

Steve, eager to connect the dots, chimed in. "So, they're also joining forces with BeTells, correct?"

"Exactly," Lucas affirmed, nodding. "But that's just the tip of the iceberg. Aligning with BeTells as a fitness influencer is more than a partnership; it elevates their mission.

Our Champions aren't just participants; they're architects of their destiny, crafting competitions, forging teams, and mentoring the next wave of influencers."

The room was steeped in a newfound appreciation for the depth and breadth of the Champion role within thrivXR. Lucas's explanation transformed the concept from an abstract idea into a beacon of inspiration. Here, in the nexus of innovation and ambition, the Champions were envisioned not merely as participants but as pioneers on a quest to redefine the landscape of fitness and influence.

As the meeting adjourned, the team left Escape Control Central with a renewed sense of purpose and a clearer vision of the road ahead. The journey of thrivXR, powered by the spirit and dedication of its Champions, was on the cusp of transforming the fabric of fitness and personal branding. In this transformation, each Champion, with BeTells as their platform, was empowered to champion not just their legend but the very essence of what it meant to lead, inspire, and thrive in the modern world.

"That's a really well-rounded and programmatic opportunity that doesn't exist now for personal trainers, actors, and athletes. BeTells will be a game changer for these aspiring Champions are going to have," Coco remarked, a twinkle in her eye, noticeably impressed and charmed.

"Exactly," returned Lucas. "What I envision is Champions becoming masters of their craft and having a magnetic orbit around which

other aspiring fitness influencers get inspired by. This is why a thrivXR Champion membership is designed to help Champions take control of their personal fitness programs. As BeTells Champion, they become member-leaders, and they lead flights."

"Uhh..Flights?" asks Coco.

"Right. The Classes are called Flights, composed of 12 Champions lasting 24-48 minutes each. The focus of each Flight will be on core stability, functional strength, and cardio endurance. Each Champion leader will lead classes of 12 Champions per class, or per Flight, if you will. Once a member, a person will sign up for what we are calling a Quest."

"Sounds epic," noticed Steve. "How do you see the program working?"

"Champions will be gamifying their workouts on our state-of-the- art XR machines to get the optimal workout. Take the Trial by Core, which lasts for 24 minutes. There's XR Yoga, which spends eight minutes on Core, XR Kickboxing, which spends another eight minutes on Core, and XR Flying which spends eight minutes on Aim. We will also have Virtual Blitz, which includes XR Flying for six minutes on what we call Power Up,

XR Kickboxing for an additional six minutes on Mitts, AI Boxing for eight minutes on WBL Champion, and finally XR Arena for eight minutes on Rhythm Master. This one clocks in at 30 minutes, so a little longer than the Core one. We also have a really fun and unique one called the Zombie HIIT. This workout includes AI Boxing for eight minutes on Zombie Attack, eight minutes of XR Kickboxing on Sparring, and eight minutes for XR Arena on Dead Zone Zombies, totaling 24 minutes."

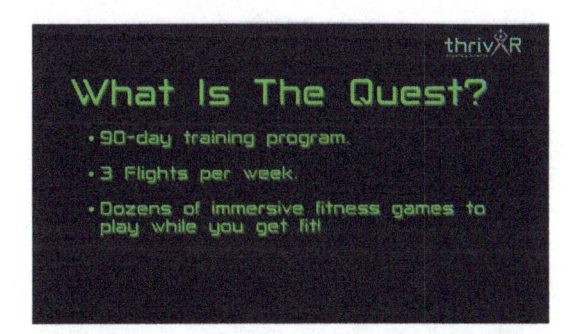

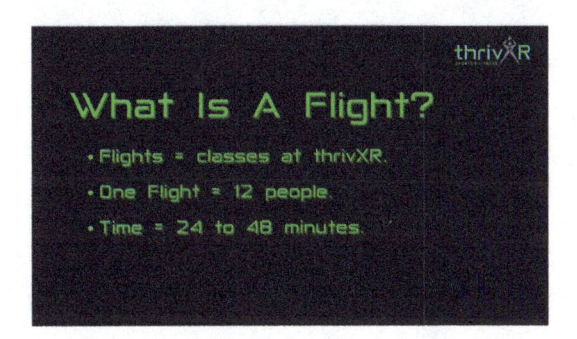

The Quest: Future of Group Fitness

What Is The Quest?
- 90-day training program.
- 3 Flights per week.
- Dozens of immersive fitness games to play while you get fit!

What Is A Flight?
- Flights = classes at thrivXR.
- One Flight = 12 people.
- Time = 24 to 48 minutes.

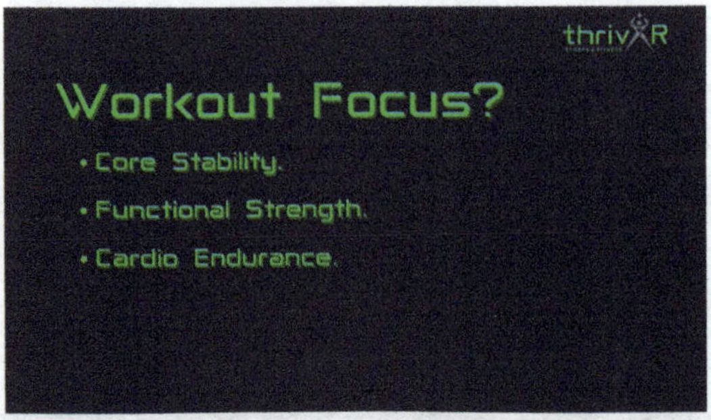

Workout Focus?
- Core Stability.
- Functional Strength.
- Cardio Endurance.

TRIAL BY CORE

What's the workout?
- XR Yoga: 8 mins on "Core"
- XR Kickboxing: 8 mins on "Core"
- XR Flying: 8 mins on "Aim"

Total Time Elapsed: 24 Mins

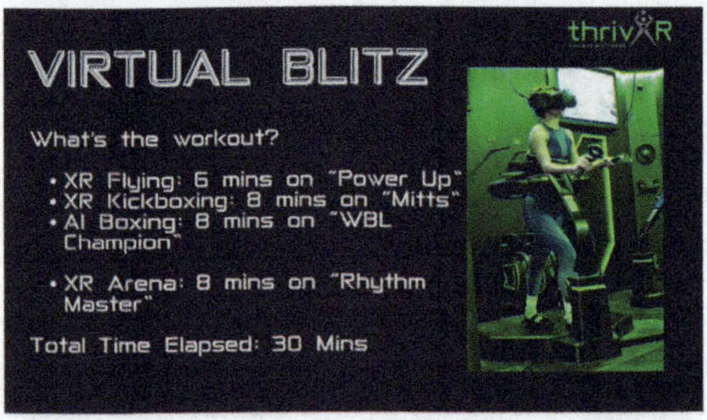

VIRTUAL BLITZ

What's the workout?
- XR Flying: 6 mins on "Power Up"
- XR Kickboxing: 8 mins on "Mitts"
- AI Boxing: 8 mins on "WBL Champion"
- XR Arena: 8 mins on "Rhythm Master"

Total Time Elapsed: 30 Mins

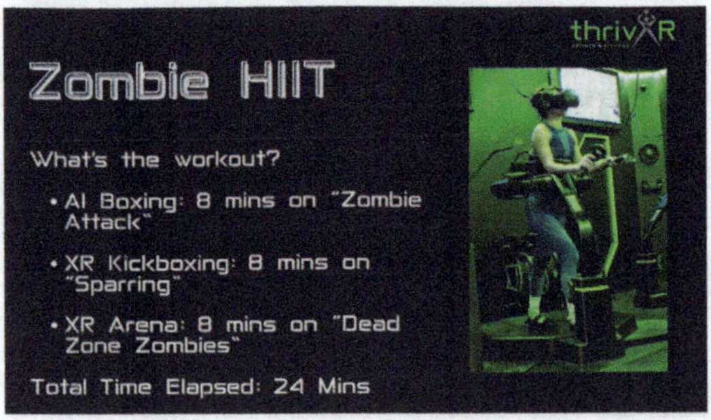

Zombie HIIT

What's the workout?
- AI Boxing: 8 mins on "Zombie Attack"
- XR Kickboxing: 8 mins on "Sparring"
- XR Arena: 8 mins on "Dead Zone Zombies"

Total Time Elapsed: 24 Mins

QUEST ALPHA
MWF AT 6AM & 7AM

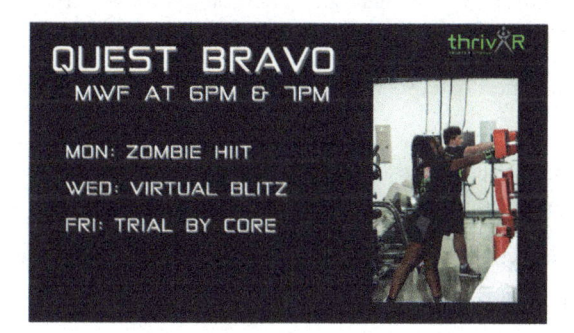

MON: VIRTUAL BLITZ
WED: TRIAL BY CORE
FRI: ZOMBIE HIIT

QUEST BRAVO
MWF AT 6PM & 7PM

MON: ZOMBIE HIIT
WED: VIRTUAL BLITZ
FRI: TRIAL BY CORE

"That sounds so fun. I may just want to try it out for kicks!" Steve exclaimed with excitement.

"Yeah..I'll believe it when I see it," taunted Coco.

"Yeah, yeah, I know I'm not a gym rat or anything, but these sound like so much fun; it's probably the only way I'll ever get to working out!" Steve returned.

"And it's going to be a lot of fun for sure," added Lucas. "There are going to be 36 Flights over a 90-day period. We will have them on Mondays, Wednesdays, and Fridays, or Tuesdays, Thursdays, and Saturdays, and at specific times. There will also be a program or syllabus that everyone will go through and be exposed to. Champions will train to win and compete in several different fun XR competitions we'll have."

"Love it!" Steve shouted out. "So, we're basically telling Champions that they can take their fitness and entrepreneurial journey to the next level, right?"

"Exactly."

"So, to reiterate," Coco said, "the Quests are going to be a 90-day period that have three Flights per week and involve Champions participating in dozens of immersive fitness games that are going to be as fun as they will be effective at getting fit, right?"

"Bingo," Lucas affirmed. "Everyone participating in the Quests gets to first go on a Journey, which is essentially a private one-on-one individualized consultation and fitness assessment with one of our in-house coaching experts. This allows us to better understand their goals, interests, and lifestyles. We deliver the gentle quench of parental decision-making with the guidance we provide."

"Champion, Journey, Quest…it all sounds so epic," Steve remarked. "Yeah, because it is! We are on the leading edge of possibility within

the Realm of Fitness here, so we wanted to match the lingo to reflect what we are offering."

"I can get behind that," Coco added.

"Oh, and did I mention there are five modalities in total? Nutrition, Cardio, Strength Training, Mobility & Flexibility, and Core Stability. These will provide our Champions with a well-rounded formula for exceptional success."

Coco's ears perked up. "What's the nutrition element involved?"

"It helps our Champions discover how to eat specifically for their unique profiles by setting safe and effective macronutrient goals. Applied knowledge is power, and we want to take them through a calorie-by-calorie nutrition plan that matches exactly what will work best for them."

"I like it. Quite holistic," Steve returned.

"Glad you do. And yeah, for the other four, overall, with Cardio we want to help Champions maximize their results, Strength Training will help them build muscle and burn fat, Mobility & Flexibility help unlock potential, and Core Stability makes everyday life easier through improving posture and balance, increasing stability, and strengthening the spine."

"Have fun and get results, right?" Steve interjected.

"Exactly!" Lucas replied. "It's all about attracting results you can see and feel while having fun doing so."

"Gamifying workouts through emerging technology. We're not just on the cutting edge; we're crafting it," Coco remarked, her enthusiasm palpable. "It's like those secret projects I was part of are coming to life, but this time, it's transforming fitness."

Lucas, ever the visionary, couldn't contain his excitement.

"Absolutely!" he burst out. "What we're offering goes beyond ordinary fitness. It's an XR adventure that marries the intensity of kickboxing, the serenity of yoga, the endurance of cycling and running, and the balance of core stability training. And it's not just about getting fit—it's about embarking on a Quest that's as thrilling as it is beneficial. We've even enlisted elite coaches to ensure our Champions' journey is nothing short of epic."

Coco, leaning forward, her curiosity now in overdrive, pressed for more. "You've got my attention, Lucas. Spill the beans on the tech that will power these Quests."

Grinning with the eagerness of a kid in a candy store, Lucas dove into the heart of thrivXR's innovative arsenal. "First up, the XR Arena—a marvel of technology where our Champions will defy the limits of physical space. Picture this: an omnidirectional treadmill that doesn't just let you run; it plunges you into virtual realms. Imagine sprinting through fantastical landscapes or outmaneuvering opponents in pulse-pounding first-person shooters while getting an unparalleled workout."

Steve, unable to hold back his inner gamer, chimed in with a mix of jest and awe. "Guess it's time to level up my headshot game in more ways than one."

With a playful tilt of her head, Coco teased, "I had no idea you were part of the gaming elite, Steve."

Laughing, Steve shot back, "All about that work-hard-play-harder life, right?"

"Well," Lucas said, "that's actually pretty accurate. Champions in the XR arena will burn calories while beating high scores in FPS games

where they're fighting zombie militias or robot villains or dancing to the beat in Rhythm Master. We've got something for everyone."

"Lucas, we should totally have a dance-off!" Coco exclaimed with excitement. "You know how I like watching you shake those hips."

"The feeling is mutual," Lucas said with a charming smolder. "Alright, get a room, you two," taunted Steve.

"OK, OK; moving on," Lucas started, "we've also got XR flying and yoga. With our XR flying machines, Champions can improve their core stability with controlled yoga or in epic space battles. They get the opportunity to explore scenic journeys at the bottom of the ocean or enjoy the thrill of virtual skydiving."

"That's wild!" Steve said. "I've definitely never heard of anyone doing something like this before."

"Pretty cool, huh? I wanted to ensure we keep people engaged so that they are compelled and motivated to train harder and achieve peak results," Lucas replied.

"Mission accomplished, I'd say," shot back Steve.

"Anyway, there's also the XR AI boxing. This boxing robot leverages the power of AI technology to interpret movements, allowing a Champion to fight zombies one-on-one with increasing difficulty levels, box to the beat of adrenaline-pumping music, and fight for the WBL Championship."

"I swear, Coco, I will show that robot who's boss," Steve said.

"I'm sure you will make it scream 'Uncle' someday…maybe," Coco replied with a knowing smirk.

"You'd be surprised what these twin Hellfire cannons can do.

"Oh, you mean those water pistols?"

"Ha ha; very funny." Steve and Coco shared a laugh, knowing they both enjoyed the joking diatribe.

"You two crack me up," Lucas said. "I forgot what I was even talking about."

"Boxing robots!" Steve called out.

"Oh yeah! All right, so we have three more XR experiences our Champions will participate in on the Quests. There's also XR avatar racing. This is one of my favorites because it's an immersive virtual indoor cycling experience with universal appeal from our observations. It helps people burn fat, improve heart health, and tone muscle. The concurrent training combines cardio exercise with resistance training, and the MatriX advanced display systems compare your performance on the leaderboards in real-time."

"Can confirm; I really enjoy the avatar racing," said Coco. "I'll sometimes hop on for a quick session before heading out after one of our meetings."

"Glad to hear it," replied Lucas. "I do the same, and it feels like virtually no effort because of how immersive it is. You really feel like you're in the experience of riding around in real-world environments but without all of the hassle and risks involving that."

"Yep. It's one of my go-tos for sure."

"Besides that and the others I already mentioned, Champions will also get the opportunity to hop onto one of our XR stability clouds," Lucas continued.

"With stability clouds, they will improve their code endurance and After Coco had read Lucas' Down at the Scene screenplay, her heart grew into a shining level of warmth and fulfillment like she had never known.

strength while embarking on virtual ski rides or chasing down their prey as velociraptors."

"Interesting options," Coco said.

"Hey, some people enjoy skiing down some powder while others prefer to devour their food while it's still alive. Different strokes for different folks." Lucas shot back.

"I don't judge!" Coco said with a smile as she raised her hands.

"But remember, we've got way more than these two options. In fact, we offer over 75 different experiences….everything from games to classes. So, there's plenty of diversity for Champions to choose from."

"I'll have to browse those a bit. Haven't jumped onto one of those stability cloud things yet," Coco said.

"You'd find it a welcoming challenge, I bet," returned Lucas. He paused as he seemed to search for the final component of his XR rundown.

"XR kickboxing! I'm surprised I almost forgot about that one," he exclaimed.

"No worries; it's been a long day, and we know how you get when you start getting hungry," Coco winked.

"Yeah, I do tend to get a little floaty when it's been a few hours since I've gotten some fuel in me," he replied. "So, I'll wrap this meeting up, and then we can all get some grub together."

"I'd like to, but I have another obligation after that," Steve said.

"That's alright. I guess it means you and I are going on a lunch date," Lucas teased Coco.

"Sure. I'm down!" she replied with a beaming grin.

"So, like I was saying, there is one more XR element to Quests that our Champions will participate in. XR kickboxing involves going head-to-head with our state-of-the-art boxing robot, which provides on-demand workouts, multiplayer training, animated sparring rounds, total body workouts, and skill assessments to track your progress."

"I swear I'm going to show that robot who's boss," Steve interjected, knowing he was about to hear it from Coco.

"Riiiight," Coco said with a smirk.

"Same time tomorrow work for everyone? I've got a really important meeting lined up where we need to go over the BeTells Creative Reality TV Agency."

"Yeah, that works for me, Lucas," Steve said as Coco nodded in agreement.

"Excellent. Thanks for coming today. I think I'm going to invite Y- Ali in for tomorrow's meeting. There's something AI-related I think she will want to have a say in," Lucas said with a tinge of mystery.

"Looking forward to it," Steve replied. "Take care, Steve."

As Steve left, Lucas and Coco packed up to head out for lunch. Once Steve left, they exchanged knowing glances that indicated they were both happy to have lunch together ...alone. While not dating per se, the mutual attraction to one another was palpable, even if it would never be actualized. They were best of friends. They knew each other's hearts, history, and heaven, which they cherished deeply.

<u>GUIDING LIGHT MANTRA CHAPTER 6:</u>

I have the Midas touch. There exists no force that can thwart the life force fueled by the focus of my consciousness.

Chapter Seven

BeTells Creative Reality TV Agency

Lucas was all alone, enraptured in a moment by himself. He adorned a pair of 3D glasses while standing in front of a one-way mirror that housed an automatic camera with a big screen backdrop. On the screen was a starship zipping through space, speeding its way through galaxy after galaxy. It was at that moment that Lucas was moved to perform a soliloquy.

"I'll never get away with launching this venture under my name, Lucas Disney Enterprises. If we are going exactly where I want to go, George and Walt are going to team up and come after me. I just don't know what to do…"

Coco walked in, unaware of what was going on but impressed with the scene playing out in front of her. Without exchanging any words, Lucas handed her a pair of 3D glasses to wear. They both turned and stared ahead in complete awe as they fully immersed themselves in the scene together. Lucas pressed a button, and fans immediately turned on, blowing as electrostatic sparks and bolts of electricity were zipping and zapping within a giant glass sphere. The phenomenon made their faces reflect in a most surreal way, as their hair was blowing in the wind and standing on end due to the powerful static electricity.

Lucas flipped a switch, and his iconic 'Down at the Scene' song came on. The two of them enjoyed the special moment today as the rest of reality faded away into nothingness…

At Escape Control Central's conference room, things looked a bit dream-like, angelic, and distorted–a bit brighter, misty, and garnering a luxury boutique aesthetic. Steve set it up so that Level 2 characters were being projected in augmented reality using a fog machine. So, Levels 1 and 2 became interwoven as Yolanda came into view, demurely smiling and staring straight at viewers in the room watching her but also broadcast even–yes, that includes you reading this!

"Hello there. Yes, you–the one trapped with chains," she said as she held up her arm and admired three shining bracelets adorning her. They were real-life thrivXR/BeTells competition bracelets. "So very fine and nice...they are sparkling and engaging...and fun to look at once or twice or thrice. Or more times and over again, we enjoy the chains," she added.

Steve, acting awkward as usual, decided to correct her. "Uh...that's bracelets."

Still admiring the shining bracelets on her arm, Y-Ali continued, "...that sparkle...they are elegant on our wrist...so we often forget what happens when you don't see the twist." Her eyes became as large as dinner plates, looking exceedingly dramatic.

Steve was feeling the vibe and decided to add to Y-Ali's soliloquy. "It can take you for a ride to a place you don't want to go...but then you may also understand...

That dancing within the ropes And liberty through law Takes you to a format

Of living in the Thaw."

Y-Ali popped into the frame, looking all smiles. "Opening the present, beginning every day. In the direction your passion takes you with your friends..."

Yolanda started somewhat staring at Ali, making sure to correct her. "You mean *fans*."

"...who you didn't know yesterday," Y-Ali continued, seemingly oblivious to Yolanda's remark. However, given her penchant for being dramatic, Yolanda added to Y-Ali's act.

"Enjoy the night, revel in the mystery, and begin to apply effort to the format. What are our competitors going to choose? Bracelets or Chains?" she said.

Suddenly, Buff comes into the forefront, bursting into the room as if he was just chased in but then acting like he meant to look that way, staring right at his onlookers, saying, "Compete with your geography in mind. Represent your home and the people."

Coco O, Y-Ali, Steve, and Yolanda all suddenly turned to look at Buff while he spoke as if to say, "Huh? What's *he* doing here? He's a Level 2 character!" They shrugged their shoulders and collectively decided to simply accept it and roll with it.

"Excuse me–you mean *fans*," Yolanda said again, this time to Buff. However, Buff acted completely oblivious and continued.

"You are going to find–" he was abruptly cut off by Yolanda interjecting.

"Everywhere you go..."

Coco O continued Yolanda's sentence, adding, "and begin to be a part of..."

Steve chimed in, "Something that every day..." Y-Ali added, "You'll come to know..."

Everyone spoke in unison, "takes you exactly in the direction you really want to go."

Buff took the reins and brought it all home, saying, "With respect for your talent, legend, and future, allow me to introduce to you..."

Everyone spoke as one voice, proclaiming, "From the BeTells Creative Reality TV Agency: Max Poz!"

Speaking of Max, hitting the XR machines at the thrivXR Fitness Studio was his favorite pastime. Back at thrivXR, Max was magically there again, going to one machine after the other, consecutively hitting high scores on the Flying Machine, Boxing Robot, and Omnidirectional Treadmill. He showed everyone how it was done by getting an all-time high combined score. As he saw the final score tally up, he pumped his fist in the air with an air of supreme victory.

"Yes!!"

"Max!" Lucas called to him. "That was a Super Duper Double Looper! You hit a new high! How did you do it? It seems like you keep hitting a new high every time you are on the scene!"

"I don't hit a new high every time I try!" Max returned. "Yeah, but how do you do it?"

Max responded by pretending to hold a steering wheel, driving. "Well...it starts when I'm drivin' down to the scene..."

Max loves his sports cars. Earlier that day, he drove his red speed demon down to Tasty Lane, got out singing in autotune while holding a handheld Orba, and grabbed a coffee and breakfast burrito from a nearby food truck. However, there were some...obstacles in his way. Well, more like friends he met and greeted, altogether joining in to sing in Max's pitch-perfect autotune, dancing as they sang a song by Max Pozel himself. It was all about living and thriving through his determined focus to be the stellar success story he is...with a good part of it being due to being down at the scene at thrivXR. Max casually departed as the rest of his merry band of friends continued to sing and dance in revelry before bowing out themselves.

Meanwhile, back at the Escape Control Central conference room, Steve, Coco, Lucas, and Y-Ali took their seats, with Coco sitting as close as she could to Lucas without it being awkward for the rest of the room. Alright, who are we kidding? Of course it was a little awkward for everyone, but it wasn't a big deal at the end of the day.

"Well, that was something, wasn't it?" Lucas said, referring to the bizarre interweaving of Level 1 and Level 2 realities. "But as Y-Ali so artistically showed us all here, bracelets are not only flashy real- world gear Champions get to wear, but they also symbolize the pursuit of personal and financial sovereignty by doing what lights their fire. Will they choose Bracelets or Chains? It's up to their persuasion and the particular path they are vibing and resonating with at any given time. Remember, anyone can switch from one to the other at any time. I wanted to keep it dynamic like that because I understand that humans are not static creatures and instead go through a spectrum throughout their lives...and sometimes within the same day!"

"Be a Champion and Tell the world, ain't that right?" Y-Ali asked Lucas.

"Presto. We're tying BeTells directly into thrivXR and the competitions we will be running. In fact, that reminds me of *Steer or Veer*."

"Steer or Veer? What's that?" asked Yolanda.

"Basically, it's what fitness influencers who won the thrivXR competitions will do when auditioning," Lucas replied. "It's part of the BeTells creative reality TV production we'll be doing. Our passion as BeTells is to put feathers in your cap and cash in your pocket. That's what we want to go with when we speak to our target audience."

"And BeTells is designed to find talent who are fitness influencers who can lead classes at thrivXR, grow and monetize their following, compete in XR competitions for cash prizes, be player coaches, have their teams compete for prizes, establish their own tournaments, and create a league. That just about covers it, right?" Coco said with pride.

"Yes, you nailed it on the head, Coco. Figures you know the deal, given you're a lead investor in the whole operation," Lucas told her.

"You sold me on the idea from Day 1," she replied.

"And you had my heart since Day 1," he said as Y-Ali rolled her eyes.

"Anyway," he went on, "Our ultimate vision is to become a content pole for a TV station. We're looking at an 80/20 split between reality and scripted reality."

"Explain?" Yolanda asked him.

"So, you know how most reality TV shows look like candid footage of situations and scenarios, but they are just like every other scripted show? They give off the illusion of being reality but ultimately follow the same format of actors and actresses given a script they need to memorize and act out. Reality is where there is no script. Actors and actresses are just winging it and being themselves as they would be if the cameras weren't pointed at them…or at least as close to that as possible. We want to go heavy on reality and light on the scripted reality. The 80/20 blend is what we have determined to be the ideal for what we're doing with BeTells. As a premier talent agency for XR athletes and influencers, we are serious about our motto, ' We take you exactly where you want to go!'" he told Escape Control Central.

"Blended reality…I like it," chimed in Y-Ali. It's leaning heavily on the authenticity side, which is what I'm all about."

"Sure do, Y-Ali," Lucas replied. "And speaking of multiple realities, there are more than just the two I just went over, as far as I'm concerned. There's Authentic Reality, Virtual Reality, Reality TV, Inner Reality, Non-Fiction or Historical Reality, Non-Reality, Non-Truth Reality, Non-Non-Fiction Reality, Artistic Reality, and so on."

"Wow…I never quite thought of reality in such a multifaceted way before," Y-Ali expressed, with her eyes widened at what she had just heard."

"Creative Reality is fun, isn't it!" Lucas exclaimed. "I'll say!" blurted out Steve.

"Also," Lucas continued, "all of our thrivXR Champions will automatically become BeTells actors and actresses. We're making thrivXR and BeTells intimately interconnected to maximize the success of fitness influencers who come through our doors."

"I've got to say, for anyone here who wasn't already aware, but Lucas has this amazing coaching ability where he literally embodies the idea of maximizing talent and helping others self-actualize," Steve tells the room, noticeably impressed by Lucas' thrivXR/BeTells hybrid approach.

"You're too kind, Steve, but thank you. I'm doing my best to create a sensational and novel approach to wealth creation through fitness- led self-actualization and acting. As a talent agent for many years now, I have learned to identify the unknown greats of the world and take them all the way to becoming A-listers. Even those who have had an unfortunate fall from grace have tremendous potential, as they have demonstrated prior to the bumps in the road, and I bring them back to the place where they are captivating the hearts and minds of fans yet again."

"I totally agree," Coco added. "Lucas has this remarkable ability to identify and promote talent and maximize it. I've seen him really take to heart that if you can conceive it, then you can achieve it. For him, he understands the minutia. It's a process that begins with dreaming and creating a wish, as well as creating a vision of what you want and what excites you which helps you to envision the *you* that you want to become. In this regard, I see what Lucas does as an intentional visioning wishing exercise, and the first step. I think it really helps that he's in touch with his feminine side, because it takes a certain level of empathy to feel into another person's energy and understand what would work best for them."

The rest of the room was thoroughly impressed by Lucas and Coco's high-level dialogue. It was clear to everyone that these were no ordinary people–these were superheroes...essentially. They would continue reinforcing this belief, especially when Lucas started explaining the deeper aspects of belief to the room.

"Thanks for the heartfelt words, Coco," Lucas returned. "I'd say for me, it's not that I'm not in touch with my feminine side but that I touch it too much," he said with a clever smirk.

"What do you mean 'touch' exactly?" she asked.

"Honestly, I really don't know. I always thought it was funny and enjoyed saying it. But since you brought it up, maybe you and I can explore what that exactly means sometimes."

"Yes, I think I will need you to elaborate and provide some demonstrative context for me as a willing participant," she replied.

"Sure, I think I can pencil that in–actually, I'll clear my schedule for the rest of the day and give you a private one-on-one lesson in the tactile arts I possess."

"Oh my god, enough, you two!" Steve blurted out. Their flirtatious behavior was too much for him to bear a moment longer.

"Alright, alright. Sorry, everyone; we got a little carried away there," Lucas told the room.

"That's fine; we know how into each other the two of you are," Yolanda said with a wink and a smile.

Amid the animated discussion, Lucas, sensing the moment ripe for a deeper dive into the ethos behind BeTells, gently redirected the flow of conversation.

"Shifting gears for a moment," he began, his voice a beacon of calm amid the storm of ideas, "I want to touch upon something fundamental—belief. And I'm not just talking about the garden- variety type of belief, but the kind that forms the bedrock of our very being...it's epistemology."

As Coco's earlier accolades lingered in the air, Lucas wove them into his narrative. "While basking in Coco's kind words, it struck me how crucial belief is. It's the engine of our existence, the initial spark of intuition. Yet, for some, this spark remains unchanged, a potential untapped. Others, however, embark on a journey of self-reinvention, aligning their values with their essence and crafting a 'vision wish'—a cornerstone of my approach to talent management."

His eyes alight with passion, Lucas shared his mantra: "If you can conceive it and believe it, you can achieve it."

Steve, ever the enthusiast, couldn't resist interjecting. "'If you build it, they will come!'" he exclaimed, earning a chuckle from the room.

Lucas smiled, acknowledging the reference. "A great line from a great movie, for sure. But we're navigating slightly different waters here. I encounter talents scattered across the spectrum of self-awareness and value alignment in my work. Some have a clearly defined value system; others are on a quest to find theirs. Through a tailored toolkit, I delve into their belief systems, uncovering their talents and the essence of their identity and strengths."

Yolanda, intrigued, leaned in. "So, you're essentially crafting a comprehensive profile for each Champion, spotlighting their strengths, talents, and skills?"

"Exactly," Lucas confirmed. "There's a distinction between inherent talents and skills honed over time. Both can be developed and, interestingly, they often merge, blurring the lines between natural ability and acquired skill."

The conversation had transcended the basic operational aspects of BeTells, venturing into the philosophical underpinnings of what it means to be a Champion. Lucas's vision was clear: to forge a space where talents could be discovered and nurtured into their fullest expression, a harmonious blend of innate gifts and diligently crafted skills. In this vision, each Champion's journey was not just about physical or creative prowess but a deeper exploration of self, guided by belief and the transformative power of a "vision wish." Here, in

the heart of BeTells, the mantra wasn't simply to conceive and achieve but to believe—in oneself, in one's potential, and in the journey ahead.

"What would you say some examples would be, of course?" Yolanda further inquired.

"These could be singing, dancing, athletic ability, and so on. Integrating coaching into one's professional life is something I find to be important in terms of achieving the third step, which is growing to a level of self-appreciation and confidence in your vision wish, plus your natural talents and skills, to the place where you are able to accept coaching and integrate it into your daily practice of what you do every day."

"This system and process really speaks to me," Steve told Lucas. "I definitely feel a strong resonance with it.

"Glad to hear it. I'd be happy to guide the group here through it at some point. I think all of this talk about belief also is directly intertwined with *trust*." Lucas walked over to his bag, flipped through it until he found a book, and pulled it out to present to the room. "I'd like to give a shout out to the professor who wrote this book entitled *The Nature and Practice of Trust*, Marc A. Cohen. I'm in the middle of reading it right now, and what fascinates me the most about it is that it provides the framework, logic, and landscape of thought that has to do with beliefs in others. I strongly believe that trusting others is the *only* way any one of us can grow as a person.

"I second that!" Coco exclaimed.

"Oh, and I would really like to read the start of this book to you," Lucas told the team. "It starts out saying that 'this characterization of trust is best thought of as epistemological because epistemic states

distinguish trust from other dispositions.'" Y-Ali raised her hand with a look of confusion on her face.

"Uhh...what's epistemic mean?" she asked.

"It simply means of, or relating to, knowledge," Lucas informed her. "So, an epistemic possibility is something that may be true given relevant epistemic constraints. I'll give you an example. You could say, 'Given what we know about the weather, it might snow tomorrow.' and that would be an epistemic possibility."

"Gotcha," returned Y-Ali.

"Also, as humans, we are constantly looking to understand ourselves. Being able to trust one another is the only reason we have civilization or society at all because otherwise, everyone would have stayed an island unto themselves," Lucas said, steering back to his previous focus. "As a species, we are currently confronted by a new vista of self-understanding that has a wormhole opened up to the whole universe, and it's just about what knowledge actually inherently is...because the power of AI is now confronting us."

"Did somebody say AI?" Y-Ali said, with her ears perked up. She has tremendous heart power and lives her life being guided by her heart. In fact, it's part of her core belief system. Tied into this is her innate burning desire to identify authenticity. She has put herself out there as an individual, wearing her heart on her sleeve, and has also paired her heart-centered approach to life with reading, TED talks, and education that firm up her belief in living authentically being vital to humans thriving and progressive. Coupled with this, she is bound and determined to leverage the power of artificial intelligence as a muscle and magnifying glass to obtain a deeper understanding of our authentic selves.

"Yep, AI, as you know, is becoming increasingly integrated into our daily lives and society as a whole," Lucas started saying.

"And even our social media algorithms are AI and know us better than ourselves!" Steve added on.

"That's right," Lucas affirmed. "AI has become so advanced that it can take millions of data points and construct an uncomfortably accurate profile of each one of us, to the point where it could predict what we want and when we want it. But beyond that, it is also making life significantly easier in certain areas, thanks to automation, natural language processing, and the like, while also placing terror into the hearts of people who believe they will be made obsolete because of it. Just take the recent writer's strike in Hollywood. All of those scriptwriters won against AI by getting some guardrails in place, but the writing is on the wall, and it begs the question...*what is humanity?*"

"It really does make you think, doesn't it?" Coco returned. "But I would say that AI, at least at its current state, is the amalgamation of what humans have done or can do, except it can do it quicker, more logically, and more efficiently. I still think that no matter what, AI will just be a reflection of humanity's abilities. There's a total solar eclipse here in Dallas coming up that will allow us a unique opportunity to connect with the cosmos and more directly feel into who we are as individuals and what is humanity. We should all get together when that happens and tune into that.

"I'm definitely on board with that!" Lucas exclaimed, with the rest of the room nodding in agreement.

"It's an interesting thought experiment, Coco," Yolanda chimed in. "What you are so fascinated with reminds me of one of my favorite

short stories by Isaac Asimov called *The Last Question*. It actually reminds me of you a little bit."

"Never heard of it," Coco replied, seeming a bit surprised that she had never heard of this particular story while also meaning to read his body of work. "What reminds you of me in this work?"

"I know you've got some amazing accomplishments in the realm of AI with your previous work, both the public-facing and the more top-secret kind. Essentially, it's very relevant now as it was back in the day when you knew where computers were going. And I'd say right now we're kinda at a nexus point where this short story predicted back in the '50s where computers would be getting to– where they can outpace the human brain."

"Color me intrigued. I'm all ears. What's the premise?" Coco asked. Yolanda's eyes lit up as she prepared to share a dramatic rendition of the story's synopsis.

"At its core, the story epitomizes the concept of the totality of human knowledge entering one central processor or computer hive mind. I'd consider it an AI system. The story starts out when there is a very powerful computer that assimilated everything...all of human knowledge, that is. Humanity asked the computer the age-old question *'What is humanity?'* and the computer said that there is not enough information assimilated to produce an answer."

Escape Control Central was silent enough to hear a pin drop, as everyone was completely enraptured by the story, as told through Yolanda's lens. She continued.

"So, human evolution continued at a rapid pace...exponentially, actually, to the point where human beings could become superhuman. They had remarkable abilities like self-healing, regrowing limbs,

morphing, taking on new shapes...and even mastered time travel! They were able to travel to all realms of the universe with ease. All of the information about everything humans had accomplished up until this point had been input into the computer and continued to be done regularly. After certain periods, humanity asked the computer the same question...'What is humanity?' Time and time again, it exported the same answer, that 'there is not enough information assimilated to produce an answer.'

Yolanda, the masterful storyteller that she was, had everyone at the edge of their seats. Seeing as she had everyone hooked, she kept going.

"Once every song had been sung, all poetry had been written, and all of everything else had been done, it was all integrated into the computer. Again, humanity asked the same question, and once more, the computer returned the answer that there was not enough information assimilated to produce an answer for what humanity is. Finally, there was almost nothing left to do but have humans assimilate themselves into the computer...and so that is exactly what they did. One last human was remaining outside of the computer, and they asked the same question as was asked many times before...'What is humanity?' The computer said there was not enough information assimilated to produce an answer. At that point, this last entity checked itself into the computer. At that exact moment, the entire universe went dark. A moment passed, after which the computer said...'Let there be life.'"

The silence was deafening.

"Wow...that got really philosophical," Coco responded, barely able to produce those five words.

"I love it!" Lucas shouted with glee. "See, this is exactly what I mean. AI forces us to question the very nature of who and what we are."

"I'd say our artistic creativity makes us human," Y-Ali said. "It's authentically a human expression. Now, I know there's AI art these days, and you can tell AI to write music, make videos, and do all that, but that's AI, not human."

"Well, wouldn't you say that human-directed AI artistic creation is, at its core, human-directed art? After all, we could consider AI to be 'human by extension' because humans developed it, and all of its data is from what humans created."

"You're onto something interesting here, Steve," Coco responded. "However, I think there should be a bit of a distinction, so I think both of you are right. There is creation vs identity, meaning that even though humans have created AI systems, the identity of creation is still distinct from its creators. Take a painting made by a human artist, for example. It's a product of human creativity, but it is not itself human."

"Yeah, and I would like to add that humans have self-awareness and the ability to experience emotions and subjective experience. AI can't do that. They're run by algorithms, and nothing they do arises from direct personal experience."

"Yet!" Steve exclaimed.

"Yeah, yeah," Y-Ali returned. "But they won't ever be biological now, will they? Humans are characterized by genetic and biological features that AI doesn't possess. Isn't that right, Coco?"

"Very true," Coco replied. "And let's also remember that humanity is deeply tied to cultural, social, and historical contexts, whereas AI

is not. Humans participate in societies in a deeply intimate way, form relationships, and contribute to creating cultures in ways AI just can't cut the mustard."

"Right," Lucas interjected. "While AI could mimic certain aspects of human intelligence and behavior, like let's say, writing a kickass script, these capabilities ultimately stem from human programming and design. The distinction between the creator and the creation is very important to assess if we want to understand the nature of AI in its relation to humanity."

"Y'all are gonna love AI STAMPOUT, by the way, I can see you nerding out right now," Y-Ali chimed in. "It's something I created that expresses all of this to an extent," she added.

"I'm sure we're all united when I say it's something we're all looking forward to," said Lucas. "In fact, that actually brings me to the BeTells production agenda."

"*Actually*, I'll take over this part," says a voice from someone just outside Escape Control Central's door. As they step forward out of the shadowy hallway into the doorframe, it becomes clear that it's none other than Buff Pepper, gracing the room with his presence yet again.

"Uhh…Buff?! How did y–…" Lucas starts before getting cut off.

"I think it's most fitting if I go over the BeTells production calendar for all of the fantastic and different productions we've got coming out. Plus, I also want to review all the different sponsors we'll be working with to make all of our productions possible."

Lucas realized it would be best if he just let Buff, visiting from Level 2, take the reins for a few minutes while he went forward with his agenda. "I supposed that's fine. Let's hear it."

"Yeah, let's hear it!" Steve exclaimed enthusiastically. As one of the lead investors for BeTells, he was keen to see what Buff cooked up so that his investment would turn out to be worthwhile.

"Can do. But first, I just wanted to say that honestly, from my perspective, and by mine, I mean Rene Descartes' perspective, when he so famously proclaimed, 'I think, therefore I am,' overcompensates for my artificial intelligence and discounts my feelings and passion for goodness and my ability to create art."

Y-Ali was completely dumbfounded, stunned, and livid. However, this morphed into depression and despondency in the blink of an eye. Then, with an almost unrecognizable spark, she busted out a dance move that was all her own right there in Escape Control Central. Her heart was enraptured with passion, desire, and romantic love for Buff. However, at that very moment, with that recognition, Y-Ali became livid once again because she realized that she was actually, authentically in love with a robot!

"Hey, Y-Ali, you OK?" Buff asked her.

"Yeah, yeah, I'm fine," she returned pensively.

"Alright, so I have two seasons mapped out for the BeTells production. There's going to be 13 episodes in each season, and each BeTell produces a quarterly episode. We're going with *Down at the Scene* as the working title for the first production and *Bounty* for the second. We're also producing *Sunglasses with Coco*, which actually is technically going to be written and produced by Coco herself."

"I've already gotten started...halfway through the script," Coco said, ensuring everyone knew she was no slacker (as if there was ever any doubt).

"I am also spearheading a book adaptation, written and produced by Lucas, called *Code of Bounty*."

"Uhh...why do I feel a sudden sense of deja vu *Inception*-style?" Y- Ali asked, feeling very peculiar all of a sudden.

"No reason," Buff quickly managed to say. "Anyway, we're also going to have the Max Poz TriArtelon, produced by Y-Ali and written by Lucas. We'll also have the thrivXR TriBoxalon, written by me and–"

"And Romeo & Juliet in Family Therapy, produced by moi!" Coco shouted out.

"Haha, yep. That's a fun one, isn't it? Steve and Lucas are writing that one. Little-known fact amongst the group here is that Steve is actually not just a tech genius but a comedic one as well," Buff told everyone.

"Well, I definitely find it comedic when he's always threatening to work out," Coco smirked as Steve gave her a knowing glance while feeling a bit awkward. "I KID!" she said emphatically while looking towards Steve. "Steve really is a genius in many ways," she added.

"Since I've been called out, I'd like to take this opportunity to pitch my idea. You might think it's a bit outrageous, but hear me out," Steve started saying. "You might still think I'm a genius or absolutely bonkers."

"You've got me in suspense," Coco replied.

"Alright, what if we just Willy Wonka the BeTells launch with a huge scavenger hunt so that competitors can gain entry to the Big Bounty Triboxalon by going the tryout and scavenger hunt reality TV path. I know it's an outlandish idea, but I think it would be glorious."

"Steve," Lucas started saying, "I love your ideas, as eccentric as they are at times, but we're in a bit of a time crunch at this point, and it would likely result in us biting a bit more than we can chew. Love the concept, though! We can put it on the back burner and maybe do something with it down the road."

"Loud and clear," Steve replied. "Thanks for considering the idea. I'll think of how we could incorporate it into a future competition in that case."

"That's a pretty rad idea, Steve. Would love to see it happen. But Lucas is right. It's a bit too much this late in the game." Steve nodded and gave a thumbs-up.

"Anyway," Buff continued, "we'll also have Free Tryouts Reels. This is a BeTells Service to Champions that Coco will produce and write by Steve and Lucas. The same goes for Your Version Actual Real Reel in Our Format of Reality TV. I know that's a mouthful but we're still workshopping the title. And finally, there's AI STAMPOUT–Actual Unreal AI Flipback, completely written and produced by Y-Ali."

"That's right, y'all!" Y-Ali shouted out as the room laughed.

"Haha, yeah, we all love your creative genius, Y-Ali," Steve remarked.

"With regards to the funded production agenda, I think it's important for everyone in this room to know that Steve and Lucas made an agreement, which Coco brokered, for Steve to provide a one-time payment of one billion dollars on June 22, 2020 to fund the production of the BeTells library, to be released in 2028. For her lovely help in brokering this deal, Coco receives a 51% controlling interest in each of the shows she produces, as outlined in the funded production agenda we just went over. By 2027, all 13 episodes of all programming will have been produced at our facility located at 4305 Maple Avenue in Dallas, Texas, as outlined in our detailed funded production agenda."

"What about the sponsors?" asked Coco.

"Right. So while Steve's investment is the largest contribution to getting our productions funded, we have also succeeded in attracting some great sponsors, all through ViralSponsors.com."

"So ViralSponsors.com has taken on the task of vetting sponsors and matching us up with the right ones," Buff told the group. "That takes a lot of the work out of the picture for us so that we can focus our collective creative genius on curating and creating the best possible productions!" Everyone in the room started clapping with satisfaction and excitement, as Buff sure knew how to amplify energy within a room.

"This is all great, Buff," Lucas told him. "I've gotta say, I was obviously surprised when you waltzed in here, but I can't say I'm too surprised that you actually have some great ideas."

"What can I say...great minds think alike," Buff replied with a wink. Hey, Buff, mind if I get up there?" Lucas asked.

"Not at all. This is your domain, anyway. I didn't mean to just barge in like that, but I just suddenly found myself here, as if I was meant to be here, right now," Buff returned.

"That's all good, Buff." Lucas got up from his chair and went over to the whiteboard, taking a market into his hand as he began to write something.

"I'm going to go check on something. Be back in a little bit," Coco told Lucas before getting up from her seat and exiting the room.

"K," Lucas mumbled without turning around, noticeably intensively focused on what he was doing.

Coco walked down the hallway, further and further…feeling into her internal orientation. She stopped for a few moments until she felt it. She knew where to go. She entered an unassuming room down the same hallway to find a familiar scene. It was where she walked in on Lucas having a moment with the universe…and where they shared their special moment. She walked over to the camera that was there from earlier, and accessed its storage by connecting it with a USB cable to a laptop sitting on a table on the side of the room. It didn't take long for her to find the recording of the moment she shared with Lucas earlier.

Coco felt compelled to play the recording in reverse as a highly intuitive person. What she noticed completely surprised her. The beginning of the recording started out even earlier than she thought it would, when Lucas gave his soliloquy. Her heart was deeply touched by the words she then heard on the recording.

"Oh, how I love Coco at my deepest core…all the way throughout my entire being. When we were kids, Coco would always call me her snuggly Socco…"

Yes, Snuggly Socco. The connection and bond between Lucas and Coco goes back… way back.

To understand the origins of BeTells, you must understand the growing relationship between these two and where it all began.

As far as BeTells is concerned, Steve sat down with Lucas around five years after Lucas graduated from college. He went to Stanford at the time, which made a deep impression on his vision for what he wanted to do in the future. After returning to Dallas from Stanford, he immediately jumped on the idea of competing with LA. At Stanford, Lucas spent a great deal of time going to all the happening spots in the city and cutting deals left and right.

VID-SKIT FACE OFF

Romeo & Juliet Vid-Skit Face-Off:

Video editors/producers compete with Vid-Skits that deliver interactive viewer experience!

If you're a video editor or producer, there's a new competition that tests your creative and storytelling skills. It's the Vid-Skit™ Face Off: a competition between video editors utilizing a new format called the Vid-Skit™. The Vid-Skit™ combines 10 video vignettes using live actors into an interactive viewer experience.

Each Vid-Skit™ will contain 2 decisions that direct the viewer along alternate plotlines and provide 4 different conclusions for a maximum play time of 10 minutes per plotline track.

The video editor, also called a Champion, selects 10 vignettes, from 40 available, provided by Max Poz Studios. The video editor then applies graphics, subtitles and a sound track in order to create a story.

The Champion must re-cut, lay in original video, graphics, subtitles and a soundtrack to each of 10 vignettes that they have chosen. The 10 re-cut vignettes are then uploaded into a custom app that prints the official Vid-Skit™ entry.

Fans will be required to commit a minimum of $10 to a bank account that will be deployed to support the Vid-Skit™ entries and causes of their choice.

It's an artsy, fun and creative way to use your video editing skills.

This describes the Vid-Skit Face Off competitions for the BeTells champions.

VID-SKIT UPLOADER

Each Vid-Skit entry has four plotlines and each plotline has two decisions.

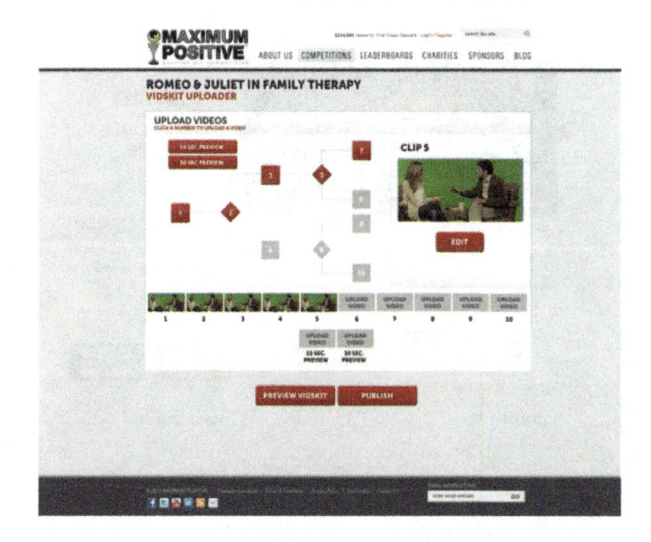

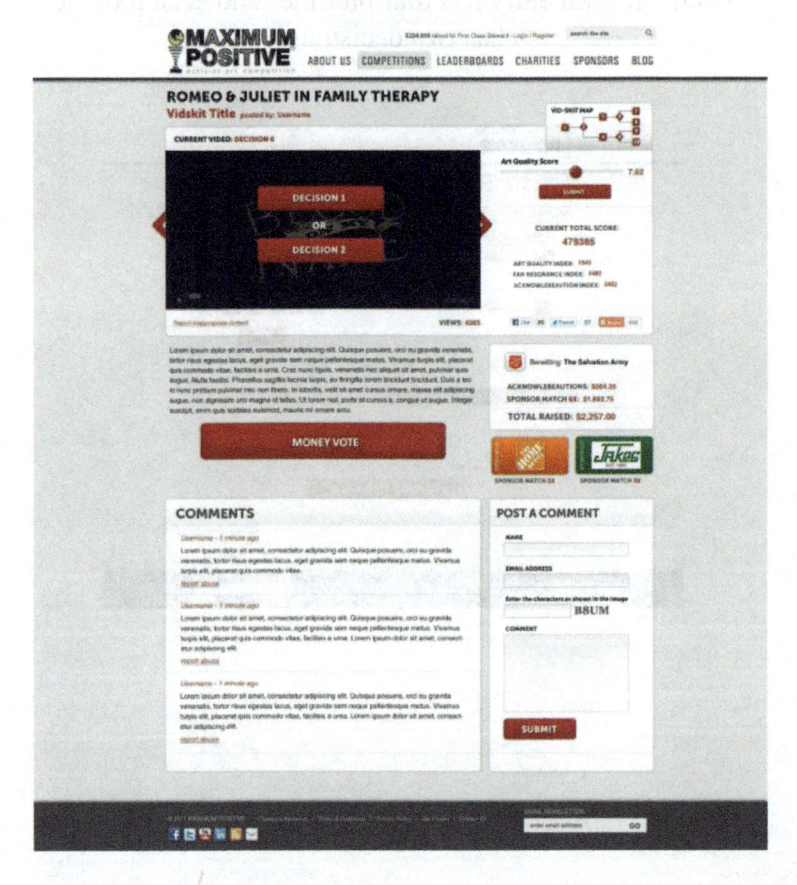

He was on what you could call a shortlist to be in an inner circle to work with major studio heads to choose who to work with from a casting perspective. This meant being in a very key position. Pairing nicely with this were many skills necessary to cast well. During one of the deals he was getting done with talent agencies, he ran into Coco.

The basic elements of getting agreements finalized, contracts signed, and all the rest were easy as pie for Lucas. After all, he watched his parents do it since he was a kid and naturally fell into it. He believed a lot of people from LA would actually do better in Dallas. Given how saturated the market in Los Angeles is when it comes to actors, it made sense and would prove to be true.

Lucas shared his thoughts with Coco over time, including his vision of what he wanted to achieve and accomplish for what would become the BeTells production agenda. Little did he know that Coco would cross-pollinate with someone who would become his lead investor in the entire operation--Steve Yabbs.

While on the red carpet circuit, Coco was repeatedly bumping into Steve Yabbs. It was synchronicity after synchronicity that just couldn't be ignored. As a highly intuitive and wise person, Coco followed her guidance, which would end up being instrumental in the success Lucas would end up achieving. Steve was a very early and primary investor in Apple Computer, meaning he had done really well and was, in fact, one of the wealthiest Americans. At Coco's third red carpet win, she ended up having a sort of back-of-the- napkin conversation with Steve, where they discussed potentially working together. Steve had a profound interest in what was happening in Silicon Valley, mostly in a leadership-oriented way, as he saw himself as a thought leader. This led to Coco and Steve establishing an initial idea of an investment vehicle, and since Coco certainly did not want to lose any time, she took it as soon as the opportunity struck. She wasted no time. She arranged for Steve and Coco to meet in her own crafty and subtle way. That initial meeting of the minds sparked the dawn of everything that came after it.

The relationship between Lucas and Coco may have ignited more recently, but the connection between these two goes much further into the past. Lucas' father was actually Coco's agent, and Coco was his client. This is a layer of their relationship that needs to be acknowledged in order to understand the...complex nature of their relationship later on. After all, they were "just friends," but the sexual tension and romantic feelings they both had for each other were undeniable.

Lucas' father saw the immense talent within Coco, yet also understood how young people are. After all, the human prefrontal cortex, the part that is in charge of planning, prioritizing, and making good decisions, is not fully developed until we are around 25 years old. This is why he told Coco that he would act as her agent and take her on as his client. Lucas' father also gave her the idea that she must put her own vehicle in place. This seeded idea would help her gain the confidence needed to be a successful star.

Back at the red carpet event, Coco had a conversation with Steve based on this idea, as her agent had suggested. Afterward, she spoke with Lucas' father, as well as Lucas himself.

Lucas had previously confided in Coco about where he would like to go as a talent agent. This was when he shared the thrivXR concept with Coco.

After Lucas graduated, he moved back to Dallas, where he ended up meeting with Steve after the last round of the Oscars. Steve happened to have a penthouse in downtown Dallas and moved there. Well, it was one of his residences, at least. He would regularly come into town and met with Lucas several times. After the thrivXR concept materialized into a real-world facility, Steve visited it several times and even helped architect the launch. It was Steve who pointed out to Luke that this is all about talent, and that he needs to have talent operating within the boutique fitness industry. It was a revolutionary concept that was not being leveraged in the industry at the time...at least not to this degree.

This is what his guidance told him. This motivated Steve to tell Lucas that he needed to create a BeTells Creative Reality TV Agency, and this is exactly what Lucas did. After revealing his BeTells presentations to Lucas, centered about the "Dominant Brand of Cool," Lucas decided to run with it because the vision he saw was possible to actualize. He also knew Steve's deep background in advanced emerging technologies and wanted to harvest the value of that technology. Steve had several ventures that became leading tech companies, so he had quite a lot of gravitas as an investor. Lucas was always keen to hear his insights, given that someone like Steve is one in a million.

The sequence of events connected Coco, Lucas, Lucas' father, and Steve all came together in a perfectly orchestrated way that helped leverage the skills, talent, and vision they all had, which directly resulted in the establishment of a revolutionary boutique fitness studio and creative reality TV agency that would make waves throughout the entire industry.

GUIDING LIGHT MANTRA CHAPTER 7:
Once I commit to stand for my cause, whatever that cause may be, my self-confidence will be forever fortified, and the universe will amplify my message.

Chapter Eight

You're Not Living Until You're Giving

Lucas stood in front of his trusty whiteboard, pondering and scribbling as Max sauntered in. Lucas looked up, a bit surprised, and with a look of bewilderment on his face, as he thought, "It is unbelievable that this is the fictional guy I created!" It was getting a bit crowded in Escape Control Central with notables from all three levels present.

"Oh hey, Lucas," Max greeted. "For now, Buff Pepper and Coco Twain are living their AI Bot lives out under the hood of the alternate universe being generated by Steve's massively parallel computer. So, they will continue to contribute from the flat panel screens. But I was able to occupy this Tesla robot in the real world."

"Hey yourself, Max. Am I not keeping you busy enough working out and setting records?" Lucas asked him. Max sat down, making himself at home.

"Well, watching you as the Gepetto of this gig has inspired me." "Go on," Lucas gestured while taking a seat himself.

"Along with the Triboxalon, what if we added another competition with videos? From everything I've seen, BeTells has SO much to offer creatives. And wouldn't it be cool to layer in another facet for the competitors as influencers?"

Lucas nodded, still wondering how his mythical character and AI android marvel became so damn smart.

"Sweet. So, here's how it works: It's called the Vid-Skit™ Face Off. It's a competition between video editors using a new format called the Vid-Skit™. It combines 10 video vignettes using live actors into an interactive viewer experience."

Max then picked up the remote on the table and flipped on the flatscreen monitor on the conference room wall. Lucas gave him a "How the heck did you do that?" kind of look. This blended reality was over his head (or maybe it was because he hit his head), but nevertheless, he just rolled with it. At the very least, he figured it would lead to some creative insights into the BeTells productions.

"A buddy of mine and I mocked up a few screens to show you what it will look like," Max told Lucas. Here is the profile page for each of the Champions in the competition."

Max handed over a printed sheet showing off a mockup he was quite proud of. Even Buff glanced over at it and raised his thumb in approval.

"I'm loving what I'm seeing here," Lucas told Max.

"You think that's cool; wait til you see this." Max pressed a button on the monitor's remote again to pull up something he believed would really impress Lucas. "Here's the Vid-Skit Uploader. Great, huh? Each Vid-Skit™ will contain two decisions that direct the viewer along alternate plotlines and provide four different conclusions for a maximum play time of 10 minutes per plotline track. Here, you can see *Romeo & Juliet in Family Therapy* as my example."

"Steer or Veer!" Steve yelled out. "You're not gonna believe this, Max, but we were just talking about that earlier. Well, in passing, at least."

"No way! Great minds think alike, eh?" Max said with a laugh. "That's what I said!" Buff quickly interjected.

"I am so confused, but in a way, it all makes complete sense," Lucas said. He figured the multidimensional display had some sort of mind-meld reality at play, which was likely explained by some bizarre quantum physics interpretation, such as quantum entanglement.

"I like having not just one or two but four different endings," Steve said. "It kind of reminds me of those old-school 'choose your own adventure' books, except here we'll have Champions who will face off in the skits and make the decisions."

"Yeah, I'm pretty proud of that," Max added. "Anyway, the video editor, also called a Champion, selects 10 vignettes out of 40 available, provided by Max Poz Studios." Max was sporting his charming and confident look, a la Patrick Mahomes, as he proudly shared that tidbit with Lucas.

"Max Poz Studios, huh?"

"Yeah, why not? It's my idea, isn't it?" Max clicked on the remote again to change the screen. "So, anyway, the video editor then applies graphics, subtitles, and a soundtrack in order to create a coherent story."

"I'm with you so far. Go on."

"The Champion must recut, lay in the original video, graphics, subtitles, and a soundtrack to each of 10 vignettes that they have chosen. The 10 recut vignettes are then uploaded into a custom app that prints the official Vid-Skit™ entry."

"It's quite innovative; impressive. And what's the Money vote button for?" asked Lucas.

"I'm glad you noticed that," Max said excitedly. "Just like the competition to choose the Max, meaning myself and Coco Twain characters, viewers will go online and vote on a screen like this. The basis for the competition is what I'm calling *"money-votes."* Fans will be required to commit a minimum of $10 to a bank account that will be deployed to support the Vid-Skit™ entries and causes of their choice."

"Gotcha! So this is a sort of anti-bot measure and a way to prevent manipulation and vote fixing. Because I really want to make sure we are making this competition as fair as possible." Lucas returned.

"Sort of. The money votes are only applied by actual people. It's art, and only people can decide who the winner is. Money votes will be strictly limited to a maximum number per person per competition. I designed the system in this way so that nobody can buy a winner."

"Excellent," Lucas replied. "And when you said *causes*, did you mean *charities*?"

"Yeah! You didn't think Max Poz Studios and the winners would bank all off the money, did you? I like to say that 'you're not living until you're giving' because giving is fundamentally satisfying. I follow an abundance mindset where when I give, it comes back to me, and then some."

"Can you explain?" Coco asked Max.

"Sure! I see giving back as being able to maximize our happiness and well-being. Donating to charities can significantly improve the lives of others, which increases the total amount of good in the world. I also believe it's our moral duty to give back, and not to do it for personal gain or recognition, but because it makes the world a better place by reducing the suffering of those in it. When we give, we also express generosity and compassion. I'd say it's actually less about the act itself and more about what it says about our character and development toward a self-actualized state of consciousness–but of course, the act makes a fundamental difference in the lives of others.

Giving also makes us feel more interconnected with the collective consciousness of humanity. If we are all part of a vast and complex interconnected matrix of consciousness, then everyone is affecting everyone else–all the time. So, when an act of good, like charity, is done, it's like the Butterfly Effect where that good deed makes ripples across the ocean of consciousness, we are all a part of."

"Wow, Max. This is very impressive," Lucas said. "It aligns with my idea of Takers, Fakers, and Forsakers on one end of the spectrum and Goers and Thrivers on the other. I believe that to be successful, and I mean *really* successful and connected with the thrivXR community, you will want to be a giver and be open to being in the flow, as well as taking care of yourself and others. After all, you need to take care of yourself if you want to effectively take care of others. Takers, Fakers, and Forsakers are playing angles and they just wouldn't fit in with the community we're looking to build."

"Love that addition, Lucas," Max returned.

"Yeah! And you just blew my mind, Max," Y-Ali said as she used her hands to pretend her head had exploded in slo-mo.

"Thanks!" Max returned, feeling satisfied he had made a maximally positive impression on everyone in the room.

"That phrase, 'you're not living until you're giving,' is pretty bold. Can you unpack that a little bit more for us? I don't disagree with it on the surface but am curious how you would describe it in greater detail," Lucas said.

"I'd be happy to. This is the sort of thing that you could say forms the basis of what I am as a person, or I guess, a fictional manifestation of your subconscious self. At its core, it means that you don't feel like you are living a fulfilled and meaningful life until you are giving in some way to someone. There are a lot of ways to attain fulfillment and satisfaction. Acts of generosity are a big way, though. We can call it altruism when speaking within the framework of charity. It enriches our lives when we engage in it, like giving money to charity or raising money through entertaining productions that we then distribute to charities."

"You know, this is actually something I have read about from ancient philosophers like Aristotle, who helped bring the idea to the masses," Steve said.

"I didn't know that, but it makes sense!" Max replied. "I feel it is a fundamental aspect of the human experience to feel like you want to help others out. I think part of it also concerns the fact that giving and helping others increases our happiness and improves our mental health. We feel this through feeling satisfied, like we have a sense of purpose, lower stress, or a deeper connection to community. Giving to someone ultimately also gives back to you!"

"Giving also provides existential and spiritual fulfillment," Yolanda chimed in.

"Sure does," Max replied. "I'd say it's important to transcend self-centered desires and concerns by giving to others because it puts us on a path of self-actualization and discovering the meaning of life. Living...and I mean truly living, involves reaching beyond our needs and desires to address those of others. I feel that you ain't truly living until you embody and practice the virtue of giving."

"You're a bard now, too, huh?" Coco said coyly. She could hardly believe this former digital avatar was now a tall, smart, hunk of a man who could now also wax poetic. It was almost as if he was evolving as each moment passed, the more informational input he absorbed.

"Yeah, I guess that does sound like a catchy one-liner. Maybe I'll become a motivational speaker and share more aphorisms on the road," Max jested. "But in any case, I believe our lives become enriched and more meaningful when we contribute positively to society, our local communities, or even a friend or family member when we are giving. We are inherently social creatures, and our lives gain much more significance through our interactions and contributions to others."

"So, basically, you are saying an attitude of gratitude, and a spirit of giving are what give life its feeling of fulfillment and meaning?" Coco asked.

"It's a big part of it, yes. And that's what drove me to design the competition in the way that I did. You see, giving can get the ball rolling and nurture a cycle of generosity and appreciation where the act of giving not only benefits those receiving the charity but also comes back to enrich our lives, be it tangibly or intangibly. To round out my TED talk, I'll just say that the essence of a fulfilled life extends beyond just personal achievements, material possessions, and all that fun stuff, which is great, don't get me wrong! But, it reaches into the realm of social connection, altruistic action, and the act of cultivating a compassionate and generous spirit."

"I wholeheartedly agree," Lucas said.

"As do I!" Buff added on. The rest of the room nodded their heads in agreement as well.

"I appreciate you elaborating on that because I think it's important for us here, in this room today, to understand the underlying philosophy of what we are doing and why we are doing it."

"100%." Steve said.

Yolanda seized the moment, her voice cutting through the air with the precision of a seasoned orator.

"If I may," she began, her tone commanding attention, "I wish to introduce a venture close to my heart, one that intertwines the valor of our Champions with the virtue of charity."

Lucas, ever the facilitator of forward-thinking ideas, gestured magnanimously. "By all means," he encouraged, his curiosity heightened.

Yolanda, with a flare of drama, laid out her vision.

"As many of you are aware, my passion for philanthropy is not just a facet of my persona; it's a cornerstone. This excitement led me to conceive a platform that elevates our Champions not merely through their feats but through their hearts."

Lucas nodded, his expression a mixture of admiration and anticipation. "We do," he affirmed.

"The challenge, however," Yolanda continued, her voice dipping to convey the gravity of her next words, "was the Herculean task of sifting through the myriad of charities, each a beacon of hope in its own right. The solution? A curated list, a veritable treasure map guiding our Champions to the X marking philanthropic gold."

Unable to contain his excitement, Max erupted, "I love that idea!" His enthusiasm was infectious, sparking a wave of nods and murmurs of approval.

Yolanda, basking in the glow of communal support, detailed her meticulous strategy. "This list isn't just a directory; it's a compass for our young titans, many of whom stand on the precipice of civic engagement, unaware of the vast landscapes of charity that lay before them."

Lucas, caught in the whirlwind of Yolanda's passion, saw the potential for more.

"Imagine," he mused aloud, "the alliances we could forge, the synergies between our Champions and these bastions of goodwill. Yolanda, your initiative could very well be the catalyst for a new era of engagement and impact."

"Indeed," Yolanda agreed, her eyes alight with the vision of what could be. "The bridges we build today will carry us into a future where every punch thrown, every mile run, reverberates through the halls of those in need."

"Thanks for that, Yolanda. And moving back to your prezi, Max, I think we were looking at a screen with a bunch of company logos. Why are those logos on the screen again?" Lucas asked.

"Oh! Companies can get in on the action, too, and sponsor a Champion. They choose a match limit that contributes to the loot a Champion can receive. The Champion with the 'maximum positive' impact, which in this case means raising the most amount of money for charity, wins the competition." Max then clicked on the remote to change the screen. "Sponsors will use this page to upload custom art and promo codes to drive transactions and promotions for their business."

"Gotcha. So, Sponsor Registration is the page they would go to if they want to support one of our Champions. And the way we determine who the winn of this competition is will be according to which Champion raised the most amount of money for charity. I think it's great, Max," Lucas replied. "And these sponsors?"

"ViralSponsors.com will be booking the deals. For example, I was just told earlier today that they are striking a deal with an electric bike company and that this company will be funding a nationwide marketing campaign to get the word out."

"Electric bike company? That's fantastic!" Coco said as her eyes lit up with excitement.

"You've sold me. Now, tell me a bit more about the charitable part," Lucas said.

"We'll keep it legit. Everybody wins." Max then clicked on the remote once more to move to the next screen displaying the Charity Application. "This is where a charity applies to receive part of the money that comes from the votes. And the charity gets to recruit fans and votes, and then keeps 35% of what comes in."

"I think that sounds great," Lucas said.

"Yeah, ultimately, the Champion that delivers the Maximum Positive impact to charity wins the competition, but everyone makes money. That's the beauty of it. And speaking of Maximum Positive, I like using the analogy of a black hole's impact on a star the size of our sun. Theoretically, the gravity from a black hole originates from a singularity, smaller than an atom's nucleus. Likewise, Maximum Positive is founded upon a burning optimism-desire-value-directed- momentum to focus artistic and musical creativity guided by activists through the cauldron of the TriArtelon competitive process to create maximum positive impacts. Also, Maximum Positive will provide the super-collider for artists, writers, comedians, rock and roll bands, fashion designers, technologists, video game developers, film directors and producers, YouTube celebrities, and actors who want to focus their talent and creative energy through a value directed lens to create game-changing impacts in areas of our world that need healing. Remember, folks, we are only limited by our imagination. Artists seeking to create positive impacts with their talent while generating income can become Champions and yield the maximum positive impact on their lives and the lives of others."

"Sharing and spreading the wealth. The act of giving is also the act of receiving!" Steve exclaimed.

"Right on!" Max returned. "There are more details, but this is the gist of it. I thought now was a good time to show this to you and knock your socks off. I figure you'll want to get the rest of the crew involved. That Steve guy will probably want to whiteboard the crap out of this, and Y-Ali will be able to sprinkle her unicorn dust on it all. That's cool with me. So, whaddya think?"

Steve and Y-Ali chuckled to themselves while Lucas had a big, goofy grin on his face. It was clear that everyone was really enjoying Max's surprise visit.

"What do I think? Bam! I think you nailed it!" Lucas exclaimed before standing up and giving Max a solid high-five.

Steve and Y-Ali both gave each other a knowing glance–something Lucas caught out of the corner of his eye. This was not the first time he had seen the two expressing some sort of unspoken bond, and he intended to finally find out what was at play.

"Hey, Steve and Y-Ali, I was wondering…you two seem to know each other well, which surprised me. How well do you know one another? Unless I'm misreading things, there seems to be something more than meets the eye? If you don't mind me saying…"

"Oh…OHH. No, nothing like that," Steve said before a dramatic pause. "But–"

"But we are really close professionally…like this!" Y-Ali explained, crossing her index and middle fingers.

"Yep, we've been working together professionally for a few years now. I discovered her back then and immediately knew she was a sensation. I was all about creating sensations during that time, and there was nobody else more fitting of that title than Y-Ali."

"Ah, well, that makes a whole lot of sense to me now," Lucas said. Y- Ali became a client of mine, and I can now see the chain of events, like me linking up with Steve through Coco, and Steve connecting with Coco at the afterparty of that awards ceremony we all went to the same year."

"Yeah, I remember that one. It was so lit!" Y-Ali exclaimed.

"It was such a cross-pollination kind of day, wasn't it?" Lucas returned.

"Sure was, and so now I don't want any more rumors flying around because I was strictly a mentor to Y-Ali, and I really appreciate the opportunity I had to help her rise to stardom," Steve said.

"That's right, and I deeply respect and appreciate Steve's guidance because it did help me rise up in the YouTube world to become the 'celebrity' I guess you could call it that I am today," Y-Ali added.

"I love it. Cross-pollination leads to these sort of amazing success stories, which I also want to cultivate as part of our governing philosophy. Alright everyone, this was a great huddle. I think we're just about ready for the big day tomorrow at the TriBoxalon. We'll still go over the details for that, but let's take a short break. I appreciate everyone taking the time today to get on the same page and understand how everything is going to play out tomorrow. This is the day we've been waiting for!" Lucas told the room.

"I am SO pumped!" Buff said. "BEYOND pumped!" Max added.

"Yeah, it's going to be awesome," Lucas said.

"I'm glad you all find my ideas a major value-add. Respect, everyone," Max said to the room. "If you liked all that, I think you'll like a new competition platform I've been workshopping called The Emotional Chain Game."

"The Emotional Chain Game? Fire!" Y-Ali exclaimed.

"Yeah! I think it is," Max replied. "So, let me explain how it works. Basically, there is a grid of nine emotions, and essentially, the artists and actors would express each one of the emotions in a different scene and clip. Then, all of the clips would get uploaded, with each clip concluding with a segue into the next emotion, while the ninth clip would segue back to the first emotion. Rinse and repeat."

"Nice! I've heard of something similar to this somewhere…just can't put my finger on it," Coco said.

"Yeah, it may have been done in a few different ways in the past, but I designed it to match BeTells and Max Poz productions," Max said.

"What would people need to do in order to participate?" Lucas asked him.

"It's pretty straightforward once you get it. Each emotion box, or E- BOX as I like to call it, will last for a maximum of 2 minutes. There will be interlinking between the emotions until it loops back around from the last to the first. Character Trait E-BOXs have to plug into all Decision, Character, Trait, Situation, and Conclusion E-BOXs. Also, Decision E-Boxes need to have two alternatives that plug into all possible E-Boxes."

"And do actors need to follow some sort of pre-submitted screenplay?" Coco asked.

"Yep, and actors can submit their own screenplay. But they have to give the film crew credit. Also, they can only check out one character per time for a period of two weeks and will need to upload their video submission properly and in the correct order to help us keep track of all submissions in an organized way. I should also add that only one screenplay matrix may be checked out at a time, while dropped in graphics, subtitles, video manipulation, and remanufacturing of E-BOXs are all allowed...and welcomed! However, since we want to keep these productions to being from Champions, we won't allow any voiceovers or soundtracks from off- site talent. And as far as soundtracks go, they will have to come from Maximum Positive selections only. Oh, and each submission needs a minimum of two decision points."

"What about Champions getting help for their productions? You know, camera crews, video editors, and the like?" asked Lucas.

"I've got that figured out," Max replied. "Actors, directors, and film crews may redo E-BOXs following the direction of Champions through the Emotional Chain Game classified ads section. This section on our platform will include areas for team-building among actors, screenplay writers, camera and sound crews, and video editors. This section will also contain some helpful ideas and hints for Champions to succeed in the game."

"It sounds like an excellent addition, Max. Thanks for coming up with this. Now I am really impressed and surprised with you, given you're a creation of my imagination."

"Thanks, Lucas. I guess you've transferred some of that genius in that head of yours to me. What can I say," Max returned with a smirk.

Lucas made sure he got one more essential piece of the competition out. "While we're all focused on tomorrow's competition, I'd like to emphasize some of its more underlying philosophical components." "Color me intrigued," Coco replied.

"First things first, we want to demonstrate how competition can be authentic to others and ourselves. We put ourselves on the line when we compete with others and ourselves. Competition reconciles our humanity, which means that competition reveals our innate talents and flaws. It is my desire to see our Champions having some self- reflection to do status checks on where they are on their paths and whether they could improve on anything within themselves that will help them become self-actualized and the best versions of themselves."

"I think it's great you brought that up," Steve said. "This competition is much more than just a physical feat of strength and endurance, but also a self-improvement practice."

"Absolutely. Alright, everyone, I'm going to pop into my office for a bit. Let's all meet back here in an hour, okay?" Lucas said.

"Sounds good," Steve replied, as everyone else nodded in agreement.

"Excellent, see you all then." With that, Lucas picked up his laptop bag and left to go to his office.

Once Lucas arrived at his office, he took his laptop from his bag and placed it on his desk. He immediately started typing away at it. He preferred the solace of his office when it got to crunch time, as it did that day before the TriBoxalon. It helped him focus without any distractions. However, he started daydreaming. Visions of outer space took up the entire real estate of his mind, with some familiar characters floating around.

As Escape Control Central buzzed with the aftermath of strategic musings and visionary pitches, Lucas, the last to re-enter, brought with him a shift in atmosphere, a blend of apology and enthusiasm. "Hey gang, sorry I'm the straggler. Got caught up in a bit of a trance in my office. So, who's pumped for the mock weddings?"

Coco O, ever the sparkplug of energy, leaped at the question. "I know I am! Let's all go out and do this!" Her excitement was palpable, a beacon of readiness.

Lucas, with a gentle reminder, tempered her enthusiasm. "We can't all go—that would confuse everything and everyone," he cautioned, ever mindful of the logistical labyrinth they navigated.

Buff, seizing the moment to flaunt his master plan, chimed in with a confidence that bordered on bravado. "Yeah, well, I'm going to show Lucas how the Champions pick out their partners so he can finally let go and hand this off to me," he proclaimed, directing his challenge at Coco Twain.

Lucas, intrigued, prodded him further. "Oh, yeah? And how's that?"

Buff laid out his strategy with the air of a magician revealing his grand illusion. "Homecoming kings and queens! From high schools and colleges in both the Los Angeles and Dallas-Fort Worth areas...32 high schools and 32 colleges," he detailed, painting a picture of a grandiose selection process that spanned hundreds of miles and countless dreams.

"Interesting proposal. Tell me more," Lucas urged, his curiosity piqued.

Buff, diving into the details, elaborated on his vision. "Imagine 64 pairs of homecoming royalty making a grand entrance from across this region. That's 128 competitors in total, each duo representing their alma mater. And to weave in the thread of philanthropy, each pair will champion a charity, turning their quest for mock matrimonial bliss into a crusade for goodwill. Plus, the venue? Tasty Lane! Right next door to thrivXR."

Lucas, nodding in approval, couldn't help but echo Buff's sentiment. "Yep, Tasty Lane is our event space right next to thrivXR. Just what I was thinking, too."

The room, now abuzz with the promise of mock weddings and charitable contests, seemed ripe for a touch of levity. Seizing the opportunity, Coco Twain, with a mischievous glint in her eye, decided it was the perfect moment for a jest at Lucas's expense.

"Lucas, speaking of getting caught up, did you finally manage to escape the 'transcendental meditation' your office plants have been teaching you?" she quipped, the room erupting into laughter as Lucas's known affection for his A-squad was brought to the forefront.

Lucas, caught off guard but ever gracious, joined in the laughter. "Yes, well, it turns out the plants are quite the taskmasters. But don't worry. I've been thoroughly grounded now, ready to tackle the mock weddings head-on."

The joke, a light-hearted jab at Lucas's expense, not only broke the tension but also strengthened the team's bonds.

Buff continued. "There will be two competitions—one for high schoolers and one for the college crowd. Since it would be logistically impossible to have this all in one day, we're going to hold the competition for the high school competitors on one weekend and have another weekend for the college competitors. Each competing couple pair, if they win the TriBoxalon, will plan and implement their own mock wedding at the TriBoxalon awards ceremony. What do ya think?"

"Good idea," Lucas said. "I would also add that our competitions are like the NFL to a degree, but unlike physical sports, which only around 10% of high schoolers participate in, our platform can serve 80% of students. The big reason for this is the massive appeal of eSports these days. An astonishing 90% of students play video games today. And add in XR, which is nascent in eSports, and eSports is nascent in VR, but even more so in XR since XR leverages much more equipment than just VR goggles."

"Yeah, our XR approach to fitness is coming at the nexus point where technology can be integrated into everyday activities, like workouts, to enhance, optimize, and maximize the results and experience," Steve added. "I think what Buff and Lucas laid out for the TriBoxalon underscores the absolutely massive opportunity for high schools to increase their student attendance, GPAs, and physical fitness of their student body."

"Those are some bold claims there, Steve," Coco said. "You got anything to back them up?"

"You know I always do," Steve said, smirking. He opened up a presentation on his laptop and pressed a button on a nearby remote to display it on the screen hanging on Escape Control Central's wall.

"Research has found that when high school students take part in regular fitness activities, they have improved cognitive functions, which translates into performing better in school. Brain volume actually increases in the basal ganglia, which has been linked to improved executive control. This translates into better planning, improved memory, and an easier time multitasking. All of these, of course, are important for greater academic success."

"thrivXR makes you smarter should be our new tagline!" Buff chimed in.

"Maybe an honorary one! But what we offer has indeed been proven to improve smarts, in a manner of speaking," Steve replied. "Anyway, moving on to more benefits of working out, students who hit the gym also see their concentration and attention spans increase. One study found that students engaging in vigorous physical activity usually get better grades. Part of the reason is that when you're working out, increased blood flow goes to the brain. This, then, translates into enhanced cognitive function."

"Wait...what were we talking about?" Buff said.

"Weren't you paying attention?" Steve said, a little annoyed.

"Yeah, I was just trying to bother you by pretending I spaced out," explained Buff.

"Ha, ha...very funny. I see what you did there," Steve retorted. "Like I was saying, hitting up a gym like thrivXR provides a number of benefits to high school students. Improving GPAs is another. A study found a direct correlation between students working out and their GPAs improving. It suggests that more physically fit kids are likelier to have higher test scores because of enhanced cognitive function and concentration abilities."

"Makes sense if you think about it," Coco said. "Based on what you said earlier about the increased blood flow to the brain. I know when I eat a heavy dinner, I'm catatonically couch-locked for at least an hour."

"Oh, I hear you. I have to clear my schedule and take a siesta if I go overboard with my lunch," Steve replied. "Speaking of feeling like crap, another one is that it can improve the immune system. The healthier you are, the less likely you are going to get sick and miss school. Now, I know absenteeism isn't a big deal with kids, but missing too many days of school could lead to a cascading effect. And this ties into workouts providing stress relief and mental health benefits."

"Mental health benefits sounds like a big one, especially today more than ever," Yolanda said.

"Definitely," replied Steve, "Among high school students, a shocking 37% report experiencing persistent feelings of sadness or hopelessness, while an astonishing 47% say they feel permanently worried, nervous, or anxious. What's perhaps the most alarming is that around one in five high school students have seriously considered suicide, with one in 10 actually attempting to end their lives within the previous year."

"That is absolutely shocking!" Yolanda exclaimed. "We need thrivXR studios across the country!" she added.

"You know, I absolutely love that idea," Lucas replied. "We need to focus on our home base first, but who knows, maybe we will see a thrivXR chain pop up across America, like Orange Theory."

"Yeah, because mental health is at epidemic levels...maybe even pandemic levels," Steve added. "And studies have found going back a long time that exercising and working out are excellent stress relievers by helping reduce the body's stress hormones like adrenaline and cortisol. Workouts also stimulate the production of endorphins, our natural mood elevators. Less stress means improved focus and performance in the classroom, besides veering students away from suicidal thoughts and self-harm."

"I'm so glad to be a part of what we're doing here. We're changing the world, one workout at a time!" Yolanda exclaimed.

"Yeah, in a way, you could say are are," Steve said. "And speaking of broader and more long-term benefits of engaging in physical fitness,

it's been found that the habits developed in high school often set the stage for adult life. This means that students who regularly work out are more likely to keep their good habits as they get older, which results in lifelong benefits for their health, cognitive function, and professional productivity."

"Working out is the gift to yourself that keeps on giving, ain't it," Buff said.

"Sure is," Steve replied. "And let's not forget that the most obvious benefit is the physical improvements workouts give your body. High school students may think they don't need to be physically active because they're so young, but the truth is, it's never too early to take care of your body. It's the only one you get, so best to treat it well. When high schoolers regularly work out and take part in physical exercise, they improve their cardiovascular health, build more muscle, improve their flexibility, and reduce their body fat."

Coco raised her hand. "I've got a question. How will you determine and decide what high schools to source the couples from?"

"Well, I was thinking that we would source our kings and queens from the 64 largest cities in America!"

"That's the obvious answer," Coco said with a tone of disagreement, "but it doesn't seem too fair to me. A whole lot of America doesn't seem to be included, and we should be as inclusive as we can be."

"Fair enough; didn't realize that it wasn't going to be if we did it that way. It just seemed the most straightforward selection process. What would you suggest?" Buff asked her.

"I think we should split up our sourcing pool into four categories— Micro, Small, Mid, and Large towns and cities. And I think we can leverage AI or an automated program to sort this all out for us. We can do some online research and create a table that has a randomized selection of 16 towns and cities for each category. Off the top of my head, I'm thinking the Micro category would include those with 1,000-10,000 residents, Small would have 10,000-100,000 people, Medium would have 100,000-1,000,000, and Large would be the ones with over a million."

"You know, that's a more nuanced approach that I really like," Buff told her. "You've got a brilliant mind, Coco. You remind me a lot of my Coco," he added as Coco O blushed and smiled.

"Well, Coco Twain *is* based on me," she said while smirking.

"Great work collabing, you two," Lucas told them. "I think you workshopped it pretty well, actually. Impressive. But Buff, I think we need to keep it between schools in the Dallas-Forth Worth and Los Angeles areas."

"Seconded!" shouted out a voice from the hallway.

"How many surprise guests are we having today?" asked Lucas. "Who has come to grace us with their otherworldly presence this time?"

"It's just me!" Coco Twain exclaimed.

"Babe! So glad to see you made it," Buff said excitedly.

"Oh, by the way, Buff, since you've reviewed audition clips already to see that you'd want Coco Twain to be your partner, I think we could cross that off our to-do list," Lucas told him.

"Yeah, of course, I was going to pick her. I mean, don't get me wrong. I'm a professional and viewed all the audition clips, but she's a star through and through in my life and the world, so it was an easy decision.

"Coolio Magic Beans."

"You could say that again, Lucas," Buff remarked. As Buff and Lucas continued with their banter, both Cocos looked on.

"You wrote my line 'you're not living until you're giving,' and I give my all!" Buff said.

"I think Max commandeered that one down a level, but sure, you're not living until you're giving, but you are a fictional creation."

"Yeah, well, you are a flawed human being, yet you created me to quench your reality. Now, if you'll excuse me, I'm going to go pick out my partner for the competition."

"But isn't that your Coco Twain?"

"Of course it is! But don't we all need a Coco? Now—watch this!"

Suddenly, reality blended into the thrivXR Fitness Studio with Buff and Coco Twain interacting with the team from the flat panels. Music faded in, with the song Coolio Magic Beans started playing. Several women took part in various activities on the XR machines, with groups of two to four chatting and laughing. Coco Twain looked like a showstopping model on the omnidirectional treadmill, earbuds in to drown out the rest of the world. Buff stood far enough away to the side so as not to appear like a creeper, but he just couldn't take his eyes off her. He started getting enthralled by Coco T and began singing the Coolio Magic Beans song as an homage to her. Coco T dismounted from the machine while Buff was in mid-song and sauntered over to him, joining in on the cavalcade of sound to bring home the Coolio Magic Beans encore.

Reality flipped back on itself to the Level 1 conference room. Everyone looked a bit stunned except for Buff Pepper and Coco Twain.

"What?" she emphasized. "It's our medley," Coco T told the group.

"Yeah, if you haven't noticed, we are really into each other...like a lot," Buff emphasized. "Anyway, I am so ready for the TriBoxalon!"

Buff told the room. "Matter of fact, I need to get going. There's some things I need to do ahead of time."

"See ya there," Lucas said to him, wondering just what exactly he would see the next day, between Buff and Max being able to track reality. "But, before you go, there are still some key things to go over about the TriBoxalon."

"Alright, but I can't stay around for too long. Got the prep," Buff replied.

"Understood; as do we; but you'll want to be on the same page with us with these competition details."

"At the thrivXR Fitness Studio, we have 24 machines so that two dozen people can compete simultaneously. There are 2 banks of 6 flying machines, 6 boxing bots, and 12 slots for avatar racing. Think decathlon style, meaning there will be a little bit of time between each event," Lucas informed everyone.

"What events are those?" Buff asked.

"You know, flying, boxing, and avatar racing...in that order," Lucas said.

"Avatar racing? What's that?" Buff asked.

"It's biking, XR style. There's a cadence meter on the stationary bike pedal, which maps how fast you're going. We can even hook it up to heart rate monitors if we want."

"Nice!" Buff exclaimed.

At the heart of the strategy session, the air was thick with the anticipation of the groundbreaking TriBoxalon event. With a masterful grasp of the logistics, Lucas delineated the structure that would underpin the fierce competition ahead. "Yeah, and remember that we will have 64 competitors for each major group—the high schoolers and the college crowd. They will be competing in Flights, with six people participating in each Flight. There can be 12, but we're splitting it in half."

Steve, always quick to express his awe, couldn't help but marvel at the scale. "Really cool," he voiced, his enthusiasm echoing off Escape Control Central walls.

Lucas leaned into the conversation with a gleam in his eye that signaled he was far from finished.

"But that's not all," he said, capturing the room's attention once more. "The Champions of the TriBoxalon get to design it. This means they will get to choose from the 10-15 games that each piece of equipment is playing and performing in. People will have the opportunity to practice on those games in advance."

Nodding in approval, Buff added, "That means it's a good idea for competitors looking to get the most prepared to get into the thrivXR Fitness Studio ahead of time and make sure they've prepped as much as they can."

"You got it," Lucas affirmed, his vision for the event becoming clearer with each exchange. "And they can have one of our coaches or personal trainers help train them on scoring well."

Buff, always one to look ahead, tilted his head thoughtfully. "I'm assuming there's going to be a party after the competition, right?" he inquired, a hint of mischief in his tone.

With a nod, Lucas confirmed, "Yep; there's going to be a party and awards ceremony after the competition ends. We'll probably also have some music over the PA system during the competition to keep things hyped, but the real party starts after we crown the winners."

Seizing the moment for a playful jab, Coco, with a sly grin, turned to Luke. "Just make sure, Buff, you don't accidentally design the competition to be a dance-off. We all remember your 'signature move' at the last company retreat. It was… unforgettable."

The room erupted into laughter, and the memory of Lucas' enthusiastic but rhythmically challenged dance moves at the last company event was still fresh in everyone's mind. Lucas, a good sport and someone crushing on Coco really hard, joined in the laughter, his cheeks reddening slightly. "Hey, I'll have you know my dance moves are a hit in certain circles," he retorted, his comeback adding fuel to the fire of laughter.

"Y'all are too funny. Well, I gotta run everyone. It's been lively," Buff said. As he left, he jumped into his flashy car, taking Coco T back with him to the metaverse.

"Hey, Coco, mind if I get an errand done really quick? Got to pick up some checks," he said.

"Fine by me. I don't have to be anywhere until later this evening."

Buff made his way over to the first stop, which was to another investor. A little smaller scale than the likes of Steve and Coco, but instrumental nonetheless to the success of the thrivXR and BeTells.

"Hey, Jack. It's great to see you again."

Same to you, Buff. I know what you're here for, so here it is." he said as he handed him a check.

"Thanks, Jack. We really appreciate your support with all of this. It's down to the wire now, with the competition happening tomorrow, so this is going to really help us with the final preparations we need to make."

"I'm glad to hear it. Looking forward to it. I'll be making an appearance at some point during the TriBoxalon. Probably will miss the beginning because of prior obligations, but will definitely be there to see whoever the winners will be."

"Super duper! We'll catch you there."

With the check he was after now in his hand, he got back into his car and drove on to his next stop, repeating the process he had just gone through with Jack a few more times. Each time, he did his best to sell the investors on making it down to the competition to see all of the action. The next day was going to be go-time, and Buff wanted to make sure he was fully prepared to make the competition a roaring success.

GUIDING LIGHT MANTRA CHAPTER 8:

Becoming a champion of my special cause magnifies the focus of my consciousness to effectuate the delivery of my unique gift to the universe.

Chapter Nine

TriBoxalon for Seekers of Truth

The sun had barely risen, yet the buzz around the thrivXR Fitness Studio was electric, a palpable excitement that stretched all the way down to Tasty Lane next door. The collegiate hopefuls from the sprawling cities of Dallas-Fort Worth and Los Angeles clustered in an eager line, each dreaming of TriBoxalon glory as winning Champions. Little did they know, their journey would transcend the physical challenges ahead, ushering them into an odyssey of self- discovery that would test more than just their muscles.

A seemingly innocuous choice awaited each competitor at the entrance—a Bracelet or a Chain. Don Everyday, the astute GM of thrivXR, watched keenly, trying to decipher any pattern in their selections. Despite his best efforts, the choices remained as unpredictable as a plot twist in a telenovela.

As the competitors streamed into the studio, their diverse backgrounds and unspoken thoughts painted a rich tapestry of anticipation. Among them, a scene that would soon become the stuff of thrivXR legend unfolded.

Jake, a confident Champion from Los Angeles, swaggered up to the registration table, his gaze locked on the Bracelets and Chains. With a dramatic flair worthy of a Shakespearean actor, he proclaimed, "The Chain, for it symbolizes the unbreakable bond between me and victory!" The room fell silent for a moment before erupting into a mixture of applause and laughter.

"Umm...that's not exactly what it means, Jake," Don returned, following a brief laugh.

"Yeah, I know, I'm just having some fun. But seriously, hand over that Chain!" he exclaimed.

Not to be outdone, Chartreuse, a determined athlete from Dallas, stepped forward. "I choose the Bracelet," she declared, "for it weaves together the delicate threads of strength and grace and emphasizes my focus on thriving." Her poetic choice was met with nods of respect and a few eye rolls from the more cynical in the crowd.

Yet, the real comedic climax came when Don, in a moment of inspiration, decided to join the fun. With a mischievous glint in his eye, he grabbed a Bracelet and a Chain, holding them aloft for all to see. "Behold," he announced, "the ultimate accessory for the indecisive competitor—the Brachain!" Tying the Bracelet to the Chain, he fashioned a hybrid that left the scene in stitches.

The ensuing laughter broke down barriers, turning strangers into friends before the competition began. This moment, set against the backdrop of their upcoming trials, reminded everyone that while the quest for victory was serious business, the journey there could be filled with joy and unexpected joviality.

As the competitors dispersed, still chuckling over Don's creation, the line at the entrance dwindled, leaving behind a sense of unity and anticipation. The TriBoxalon was more than just a competition; it was a stage for drama, comedy, and the timeless quest for self-actualization, all wrapped up in the choice between a Bracelet and a Chain.

Besides being Homecoming King from the LA area, Alex was a tall, well-built college athlete. He had always dreamed of making it big in the world of competitive sports but found his path diverted by the need to support his family's bike shop. The TriBoxalon represented a chance for him to finally pursue his passion on a global stage. His deep-set eyes and easy smile contradicted his intense focus and determination to win.

Both nervous and excited, Alex was continuously strategizing as he awaited to be let into the TriBoxalon, running through all sorts of potential scenarios in his head. He was deeply motivated by his desire to prove himself. This was someone who was driven by the desire to overcome obstacles and achieve his dreams...as well as perhaps gaining a new emotional connection with the woman in front of him on the line–Jordan.

Joining the pack from the Dallas area as the daughter of Korean immigrants, Jordan was a bit of a prodigy regarding technology. From a young age, she seemed to be attracted to cutting-edge technologies like XR, and blending it with fitness was something she figured would help her get more motivated to work out—something she struggled to get herself to do.

Her small build allowed her to be agile, which would be useful for the quick movements necessary in the TriBoxalon. She was anticipating wearing a Bracelet as she blended her intuitive understanding and analytical thinking for a holistic view of what she could gain from the experience. Even if she didn't win, she would have felt victorious due to believing she had mastered herself.

As Alex looked over at Jordan and sparked some light, witty banter, Jordan blushed, finding his dedication to success refreshingly genuine. Back home, she did not have many friends who were into self-actualization. Seeing Alex's sincerity in that pursuit and his muscular physique really turned her on.

Not all who were in line were just fabulous Homecoming Royalty. Some of these were even diehard fitness instructors, like Sofia. Originally from Brazil but moved to Dallas to go to college, Sofia had a vibrant and bubbly personality and was also into innovative workout routines. She saw the TriBoxalon as an opportunity to expand her brand and monetize her following more. She was passionate about inspiring others to embrace novel XR equipment in fitness routines.

Radiant, with a commanding presence that drew the eyes of other Champions standing alongside her in line, Sofia's style was as colorful as it was expressive, mirroring her lively spirit. This woman appeared as a whirlwind of positivity and ambition to others. In her life, she was always looking for new ways to engage and motivate her followers.

The TriBoxalon was not just a competition for her but a platform to showcase her philosophy on fitness and well-being. It was why there was no surprise that she took a Bracelet. It also wasn't a secret that she was captivated by the aura of Kyrie, whose seemingly quiet strength and depth appeared to promise stories yet untold.

Standing just a few people in front of Sofia, Kyrie was demure and poised. Studying to become a bioengineer participating in the TriBoxalon may not appear to align that well, yet it did so perfectly. She was deeply into biohacking and improving human health to achieve peak performance. She viewed the competition as a testing ground for her theories on biofeedback and XR equipment being instrumental in assisted biohacking.

Commanding an athletic presence that appeared to be respected among others nearby, Kyrie favored function over fashion, and it showed in her wardrobe choices, which included black leggings with smartphone pockets, gray fingerless gloves, and a brown headband. She maintained a biofeedback device on her wrist, which was unobstructed by the Chain she requested from the thrivXR staff to wear during the competition.

Yes, Kyrie was a purpose-driven soul, intensely focused on the potential scientific contributions her participation could bring. She ran scenarios through her mind regarding the kinds of data she would potentially record during the TriBoxalon.

As the competitors prepared for the TriBoxalon, their diverse backgrounds and motivations created a rich tapestry of ambition and engagement, resulting in an extraordinarily exciting scene for onlookers. The TriBoxalon served not only as a place for physical prowess but also as a convergence point for diversity, with each competitor contributing to the multidimensional experience. Through their competitive and personal interactions, these collegiate athletes embarked on a journey that transcended the boundaries of fitness as they knew it, exploring the depths of human potential and the expansive possibilities of XR fitness.

LATER THAT DAY...

At the revolutionary thrivXR Fitness Studio, the College TriBoxalon was more than just a competition; it was the stage for an unforeseen romantic comedy that would intertwine the fates of the Trixietrue Sisters and the three Farrell Brothers in the most delightful ways.

As the audience at Tasty Lane, next door to the competition, savored potato salad and apples–the favorite eats of the Trixietrue Sisters– that just happened to be served on one of the tables set up for the spectators, their eyes were glued to the screens showcasing the event. Sara, Cara, and Farrah Trixietrue, the limber and vivacious sisters from College Station, were the center of attention, not just for their athletic prowess but for their undeniable charm.

Spotting the three Farrell Brothers for the first time, Sara whispered excitedly to her sisters, "Look at those three. They're like the answer to our unasked prayers!"

Cara, always the comedian, quipped, "I hope they like roller derby and potato salad because that's the package deal with us!"

Farrah, the dreamer among them, sighed, "Imagine the stories we'd tell our grandkids..."

Meanwhile, Daryl, Merrill, and Meryl, equally struck by the Trixietrue Sisters, mustered the courage to introduce themselves. Daryl, with a confident grin, approached first.

"Hi, I'm Daryl, the MMA fighter. You may have heard of me. And these are my brothers, Merrill and my other brother Meryl. We're more than just workout enthusiasts; we're admirers of formidable athletes…and you three certainly fit the bill."

Ever the charmer, Ferrell Meryl added, "And by formidable, he means both on the track and in the heart."

Lucas, the TriBoxalon organizer, couldn't help but overhear the exchange. Trying to maintain his composure, he teased, "So, the Ferrell brothers from Terrell meet the Trixietrue sisters from College Station. Sounds like the start of a legendary tale."

The sisters, amused and intrigued, engaged in playful banter. Sara, with a twinkle in her eye, said, "Well, if it isn't the fabled brothers. We've heard tales of your feats. Tell me, do they involve making electrifying connections?" gesturing to Daryl.

With a laugh, Daryl replied, "Only when I'm not sparking interest elsewhere. But I've never encountered a circuit I couldn't complete…until now, perhaps?"

Always ready with a witty retort, Cara turned to Merrill, "And you, a deal finder? Hope you're prepared for a partnership that's more rollercoaster than merger."

With a playful smirk, Merrill responded, "I've always appreciated a good thrill. Besides, every rollercoaster ends up right where it started, ideally with everyone still on board."

Looking at Meryl, Farrah said softly, "And an MMA fighter. I imagine you know a thing or two about taking hits and staying in the ring."

Meryl, with a gentle smile, replied, "Indeed. But the most important fights are the ones we fight for the people we care about."

As the event unfolded, the flirtation between the six became a deep connection, with shared laughs, exchanged glances, and mutual admiration setting the stage for an unforgettable proposal. At the end of the TriBoxalon, under the glow of the Dallas skyline, the brothers each took a knee, presenting thrivXR rings to the sisters–all the same kind.

The crowd at Tasty Lane erupted into cheers as Lucas announced, "Let's make this official at the high school TriBoxalon, shall we? Matches made not just in thrivXR but in the stars. You all make three perfect pairs for a mock wedding!"

The mock marriages, held at the subsequent TriBoxalon, were a spectacle of love, laughter, and a shared passion for life. The vows were a mix of heartfelt promises and humorous pledges, such as "to always cherish each other's wins, whether in life or on the roller derby track," and "to support each other through every electric failure and market downturn."

As they exchanged rings, Daryl joked, "I promise to light up your world and never let the power go out on our love."

Merrill added, "I vow to always spot the best deals in life, especially those involving potato salad and apples."

Meryl concluded, "And I, to fight for our happiness, with all the strength and dedication I have in the ring."

The Trixietrue Sisters, teary-eyed and laughing, each made their vows, promising a life filled with adventure, support, and unconditional love, cementing the start of three legendary partnerships that began with a chance encounter at a decathlon.

As the celebrations carried on, Lucas, watching the joyous scene, couldn't help but think, "Only at thrivXR could fitness lead to such a fit of fate." The event celebrated athletic prowess and marked the beginning of three beautiful journeys of companionship, proving that sometimes, love can be found in the most unexpected places and competitions.

The first pair to win the real TriBoxalon, Delilah, and Bocephus, earnestly read the script for the Level 2 TriBoxalon while in character as none other than Buff Pepper and Coco Twain. As they read the script a bit more, they started finding a groove and impressing Lucas with how closely they resembled his Level 2 creations.

Meanwhile, amidst the completely surprising proposals and marriages, an even more massive crowd began gathering at Tasty Lane. The atmosphere down at the scene was charged with the buzz of anticipation, and the air was thick with the excitement of hundreds gathered for the climax of the TriBoxalon.

Don, the GM of thrivXR, stood poised at the podium like a general ready to lead his troops into battle, albeit one armed with a microphone instead of a sword. His mission was to dazzle the assembly of reporters, fans, and competitors with an epic announcement that would cap off the event.

As Don surveyed the crowd, a mix of anxiety and adrenaline coursed through him. The turnout exceeded all expectations, transforming Tasty Lane into a vibrant sea of eager faces, each hungry for the culmination of months of tireless preparation and fierce competition.

With a deep breath, Don launched into his introduction, his voice booming over the speakers.

"Hello and welcome to thrivXR's TriBoxalon Awards Ceremony! A huge shoutout to ViralSponsors.com for hosting this event and competition! I'm Don Everyday, your

MC for the evening, here to announce the winners of the first-ever 32nd level doubles competitions of TriBoxalon, hosted right next door at thrivXR!"

The crowd erupted into a frenzy of cheers, the sound wave almost tangible in its intensity. As the applause died down, Don prepared to reveal the winners, but not before the evening took a turn toward the unexpected.

Just as he was about to proceed, a rogue drone, bedecked with thrivXR banners, whizzed past the podium, narrowly missing Don's head. The crowd gasped, then erupted into laughter as Don, ever the showman, ducked with a grace that would have made a ballet dancer proud.

"Seems like even our drones are excited to find out who the winners are!" Don joked, quickly regaining his composure. The audience chuckled, the tension momentarily diffused by the unexpected aerial interloper.

But the surprises weren't over. From the back of the crowd, a voice boomed, "Don, before you announce the winners, I've got a bone to pick with you!" The crowd parted like the Red Sea to reveal Buff, striding forward with a mock-serious scowl.

"Oh?" Don raised an eyebrow, playing along. "And what might that be, Buff?"

Buff reached the podium, turning to face the audience dramatically. "I challenge you, Don Everyday, to a post-ceremony dance-off! The real final showdown of the TriBoxalon!"

The crowd went wild, cheering and whistling at the prospect. Don, momentarily taken aback, burst into laughter. "You're on, Buff. But be warned, I've been practicing my victory dance since we started planning this event!"

The playful banter between Don and Buff, the drone's unexpected cameo, and the crowd's high spirits transformed the awards ceremony into a memorable spectacle of joy and camaraderie. As Don finally announced the winners, the TriBoxalon Awards Ceremony became a celebration of athletic prowess and a testament to the thrivXR community's spirit of fun, friendship, and unforgettable moments.

Don composed himself for his big announcement. "Anyway, besides being GM of thrivXR, I also play Max Pozel in the Buff Pepper super duper reverse looper called Maximum Positive, a Lucas Disney production. So, I am not only serving as a functional fictional character but also the real General Manager of thrivXR. Lucas Disney, our own 'King Geppetto,' has, in fact, achieved his dream of turning his fictional character of the son he never had into a real person by creating and producing the first super duper triple looper that features both a third-level reverse looper and a 32-level mixed doubles TriBoxalon!"

The crowd was really hyped by now and broke out in applause.

"Within all of the levels of both our fictional productions and in real TriBoxalon competitions, we have relied on the team's 'super duper double looper' to mean both a fictional work where the author produces a fictional work about an author producing a fictional work about an author producing a fictional work. In thrivXR parlance, 'super duper double looper' means an actual TriBoxalon round where the thrivXR champion posts record scores on each event back-to-back in the same TriBoxalon double circuit! At thrivXR, we are introducing new ways of self- actualizing and gaining independence by becoming fitness influencers. Both BeTells and thrivXR work hand-in-hand to provide a new way and leading vehicle to achieve self- actualization and wealth generation through XR. So, all you fitness influencers, former and existing pro athletes, aspiring movie and TV stars watching right now, and people who want to grow and monetize their herd, you've come to the right place!

I strongly believe that we have what it takes to actualize our mission to create the most compelling sports and fitness company of the 21st century by leading the world's shift to gamify sports and fitness with XR!"

The crowd loved what they heard and cheered once more with a thunderous roar.

"With all of that said, we have come to the time for the real newsworthy reason for this press conference where I, as both the fictional functional Don Everyday in Max Pozel's Maximum Positive production and the real Don Everyday as GM of thrivXR, award the $10,000 cash prize to the winning mix doubles Buff-Coco team!"

A wave of roaring cheers ripped through the crowd. Clearly, many had these two pegged as their hopeful winners–and they were absolutely thrilled with the result. After introducing the winning Champions Buff and Coco, Don invited them up to him to say a few words and answer some interview questions he had prepared for them.

"Congrats, Buff and Coco! Come on up here!" The winning couple make their way up to the podium with smiles from ear to ear. Buff was running up to the stage so quickly that he nearly tripped, but he did a bit of a twirl and dodged a nasty fall that would have been caused by a loose cable on the ground. Buff grabs the mic with excitement, about to speak faster than he can think.

"This woman right here is the reason I am standing before you! COCO LIGHTS MY FIRE!"

Being both shocked and flattered, Coco quickly took the mic from Buff.

"And you're *my* reason for being here beside you! WE ARE MAGIC MAKERS!"

With that exclaimed statement, Coco took Buff's hand, placing hers into his and raising it as high as they could go in a claim of victory. Buff took the mic back to give his semblance of an acceptance speech for the $10,000 cash prize they were given.

"I'd also like to thank myself for believing in myself and pushing myself to show up every day and put in the effort and training needed to win this thing. My belief in myself and Coco's belief in me is what got me to stand up here today."

"And I'd like to give a shout out to myself as well," Coco said when Buff passed her the mic. "Some people didn't think I would make it this far. But, after spending every moment of free time I had to put in the hours for training and strengthening my mental fortitude, I shaped myself into the woman I am here today, holding it down for all women who want to believe they can achieve anything."

"Thank you for that bold and invigorating acceptance speech, you two," Don responded, not knowing exactly how to follow up an act like that. He continued. "In case anyone in the crowd isn't aware, which I doubt at this point, our collegiate TriBoxalon winners today are Buff Pepper and Coco Twain. This power couple absolutely crushed it during the TriBoxalon, and it's really no wonder they ended up winning."

"Thanks, man, that means a lot to me," Buff returned. "And me!" Coco Twain added.

Don started going over their performances and scores. "It looks like you both had great strategies that involved pacing yourselves, expanding observational awareness, and knowing your way around the machines. What was your approach to winning?" Buff took on the question head-on.

"Well, winning a competition like the TriBoxalon requires a comprehensive approach that integrates physical preparation, mental fortitude, and strategic execution across the board. My strategy was multifaceted. For starters, I ensured my training was balanced and spread out across the different XR machines next door at thrivXR. I prioritized a balanced training program that Coco and I made together. I placed special emphasis on training more in the areas I was weaker in than where my strengths lay."

"Oh? And where's that?" Don asked.

"Those stability clouds threw me for a loop the first couple of times. But then I started thinking with my feet, and soon enough, it became like riding a bike, more or less. It's all in feet, not the mind. As soon as you start thinking too much about what you're doing, you end up falling. It's sort of similar to how when you think about how to walk, you end up walking weirdly and getting laughs from people passing you by on the sidewalk." There was a light chuckle going through the crowd. "See, these people know what I'm talking about!"

"Gotcha. So that's how you kept your competitive edge over the other Champion competitors here today. Anything else you can share with us?" Don asked.

"Yeah, totally. I also recognized the intense demand that TriBoxalon training can have on the body, so I invested considerable time in injury prevention techniques. I'm talking about stretching before hopping onto the XR machines, taking joint supplements like turmeric, collagen, and black pepper, and actually eating super clean to avoid any foods that cause inflammation. Also, my recovery protocol includes getting enough shut-eye every night after a day of training, going to get a sports massage, and jumping into an ice bath. All of these helped me remain in peak condition throughout my training and the competition itself."

"Great advice, Buff. Not many people consider nutrition an essential component of injury prevention, so thanks for sharing that with us. And how about mental preparation? What did you do, if anything, to get into the right headspace for the competition?"

"Yeah, Don, I did some things in that regard because mental toughness and adaptability are vital to win a competition like the TriBoxalon. I worked on managing my stress levels by doing mindfulness meditation every day during my training period, some visualization techniques, and setting goals for myself. All of these were effective in enhancing my mental resilience."

"Impressive," Don replied. "And how about managing your energy levels? As we all know and saw, the TriBoxalon is energy-intensive. How were you able to maintain your energy levels so well?"

"I was really mindful of what I ate like I mentioned earlier, and I also included some helpful supplements, like magnesium, B vitamins, and a few others, to help me sustain my energy levels. I also planned to get enough rest between training sessions and during the competition knowing when to push hard versus conserving energy."

"That's a pretty savvy strategy. No wonder you won! And Coco, let me bring you into the conversation here. Let's talk about sizing up the competition. Did that factor into the strategy you two had going into this thing?"

"Like Buff said, we both crafted the strategy that eventually led us to victory, so I did pretty much the same as Buff. As far as competition analysis goes, I found it to be very helpful to understand my competitors' strengths and weaknesses. This allowed me to strategically channel my efforts into the right places. I would sometimes adapt my strategy in real-time during the TriBoxalon to exploit opportunities where I could gain the most and lose the least."

"That's a very smart play. Nice work!" Don replied. "One more question, Coco: what advice would you give to all of the aspiring Champions in the audience and those watching live online?"

"My advice to aspiring Champions is to stay committed to your training, focus on both your physical and mental preparation, and always embrace opportunities like this one where you can review what worked and what didn't for the competitors in this TriBoxalon.

Remember that perseverance and a positive mindset are key to overcoming challenges and achieving success. I know they were for me!"

"Brilliant answers you two. So, basically, what I got from all of this is that your victories resulted from a disciplined and holistic approach that emphasized balanced training, injury prevention, mental preparation, event-specific tactics, energy management, and strategic competition analysis. It sounds like each element played a crucial role in achieving your incredible success.

Don asked a follow-up question. "Did you have any previous exposure to the XR fitness equipment?"

"Oh, definitely!" Coco T replied. "We would make a habit of dropping down to thrivXR a few days a week when we had some free time to make sure we understood how these XR machines worked and how to get to know them more than they know themselves. They're a bit different than your average gym equipment."

"Uhh...you know they're not self-aware Skynet-style, right?"

"Yeah, Don, of course," Coco said with a chuckle, "but you know what I mean. We studied how the equipment worked by trying out all of the settings, playing all the available games, and getting as intimate of a feel for how they work."

"That's what I love to hear! And I ask for your guidance since I've seen you two next door at thrivXR more times than I can remember. You know, me being the GM and all. So that's a tip for all prospective Champions out there who are considering competing. For the best chance at being the best, I highly recommend coming down to the thrivXR Fitness Center and trying out the equipment for yourselves! You can never be too prepared, and given the futuristic and unique nature of our XR equipment, you will want to at least give them a test drive before you start boxing a robot or blasting the heads off of zombies."

"Oh man, those games were so sick!" Buff exclaimed. "I'd play those just for fun."

"Yeah, they're a lot of fun. We made sure to select a variety so that we had something for everyone," Don said.

"I'd like to also say that Buff and I really helped each other win, I'd say..."

"Oh, and how's that, Coco?" Don asked.

"Well, you know what they say...you are the five people you spend the most time with, and Buff and I spent A LOT of time together. I think we reinforce good habits and behaviors in one another, which helped us stay on task and focused on being the top competitors we could be for the TriBoxalon."

"That's right!" Buff chimed in. "Coco T has been such a positive influence on my life...for this competition and a lot more. So I'd say that's right on the money."

"And speaking of money..." Don started saying, "you two have won $10,000! How does that feel?"

"Well, Don," Coco said, "it feels really fulfilling to know that thanks to our superior fitness performance today, we have been able to help out a charity that could use the money. We decided to go with the local one that helps women who have had to escape domestic abuse situations. Those women rarely have spare cash on hand to get out of their circumstances due to the abusers in their lives keeping tabs on every little thing they do, so to have such a caring, compassionate,

and helpful charity right in our backyards was a no-brainer for us to combine our prize money together and donate it to that charity."

The crowd gave a deafening cheer while clapping for Coco's speech.

"That is incredibly inspiring. Thank you for sharing that with all of us here today, and thank you for both deciding to pool your prize money together for such a noble cause," Don told them, followed by another round of applause from the crowd.

"So, let me ask you..." Don started saying to the Champions, "how exactly did you two beat out the dozens of other amazing competitors out there today? Your scores both blew everyone else out of the water by a mile."

"Well," Buff starts humble-bragging, "I've got the stability of the Green Goblin on the stability clouds...but I'm much better looking." Coco lightly pushed him with her hand while sporting a grin. "But seriously, I've been practicing–a lot. Practice makes perfect, as they say, and I have given up a lot of time where I could've been partying or being a couch potato where I was at the gym instead. I learned the moves the boxing robot had and learned to predict what they were going to be...kinda like the guy in that Drunken Master movie. I also biked my ass off on the thrivXR avatar racing and made sure to take my essential amino acids, creatine, and protein smoothies to get my body in peak performance. With so many fun XR integrations on those electric bikes, the time just flew by when I was on them. Basically, I tried out a couple of XR machines every time I went to the studio, and I'd say within a week, I would have done the entire circuit at least once."

"Thanks for sharing some of your tips and strategy, Buff," Don said. "How about you, Coco?"

"I'll also say that my approach was very similar in many ways, but I had to account for certain physiological differences Buff and I have, including my cycle and making sure I'm not doing intermittent fasting like he does since it affects women differently. But I was also giving the Bot Boxer a piece of my mind, soaring around on the flying machines, biking through majestic mountains, being glued to the stability clouds. The key for me was training and observing how others were training. Even though the people around me weren't necessarily going to be my direct competitors at the TriBoxalon, I could peer into the psychology of each person working the machines, which gave me a good understanding from an external perspective of what those people were doing that worked and what were their blind spots, so to speak."

"That is fantastic to hear. Thanks for sharing that, Coco," Don said. "Buff, any last words?"

"Yes, I'd just like to share some words of inspiration for the crowd out there based on my experience in the TriBoxalon competition. What I concluded was that competitions reconcile our inner need for meaning with performance. They serve as platforms where our inherent needs for meaning and the desire to perform beyond what we normally would intersect and harmonize. I would say there are five major benefits competitions provide us...at least what they have given me."

"Oh yeah? What are those?" asked Don.

"Purpose and motivation because of the clear objectives and goals competitions have, self-identity and validation due to being able to express ourselves through our skills and strengths, mastery and growth by pushing ourselves to our limits, community and belonging when we are all competing towards the same thing, and recognition and achievement which are incredibly fulfilling. I'd also say that while being competitive is key to winning in something like the TriBoxalon, we also have to make sure we are not making unhealthy comparisons to others, placing too much undue stress on ourselves, especially when we're training for a competition leading up to it, and avoiding having too much of a focus on the outcome at the expense of learning and enjoying the journey."

"That was really inspiring, Buff. And amazing alpha content shared here by both of you for aspiring Champions," Don said, marveling at how much the two revealed about their strategies. "These two are shining examples of what happens when you quench your best self. Thank you both for participating in this collegiate TriBoxalon competition, and congratulations again on winning! Let's give them a big round of applause, everyone!" he shouted as the audience cheered deafeningly for the Champions.

"Oh, and remember," Don added, "for all of you out there in the audience who are interested in competing in one of our upcoming competitions, I encourage you to get involved in thrivXR and BeTells because we've got this and a lot more I think you're going to want to be a part of! All you future Champions in the crowd I see out here today can become self-actualized, wealth-generating thrivers, monetizing your herds in ways that bring you complete fulfillment. If you want to experience what it truly means to thrive in this life, then drop in and chat with us. We'd love to help you quench your best self."

Don kept the crowd's attention for a little longer as he prepared to share something important about the thrivXR-BeTells crossover.

"At the TriBoxalon, our Champions are competing for a cause of their choosing. In partnership with BeTells Creative Reality TV Agency, we want you to BE a champion and TELL the world. And we encourage each Champion to use the Champion's Creed as their guiding light--Athleticism reconciles my humanity. Charity delivers my promise. Competition reveals by truth."

The crowd, especially the Champions, gave a solid round of applause before Don continued. "When you wish upon a star, you're just like those who already are. Live your creed to create your legend. Participate and Impact Now! THAT is the Champion Reality."

The TriBoxalon was a stunning success based on the audience's reaction, and the inseparable Buff Pepper and Coco Twain were star athletes that day, showing other prospective Champions how it's done. The participants from the Los Angeles and Dallas-Fort Worth area colleges, half from each region, were all giving their best. It was becoming clear that thrivXR would have to expand–first to LA and elsewhere. This boutique fitness center has the potential to follow in the footsteps of others who started small and ended up transforming the lives of people nationwide, like the famous Orange Theory.

Buff and Coco, both from Dallas-Fort Worth area colleges, actually met during the TriBoxalon competition. From the moment they saw one another, something stirred within them–something that yearned for more, and whatever this meant, each of them felt it had something to do with following those deep-seated feelings. Buff had sung what he felt was his ode to his Queen Coco–Coolio Magic Beans. This rather provocative hymn to his goddess was one of the key reasons Coco fell for him...hard. From that moment forward, these two would go on an inseparable journey to success and stardom.

With the collegiate TriBoxalon now complete, the thrivXR team, along with Champions Buff and Coco, were already planning the TriBoxalon for high schoolers who were the homecoming king and queen, or homecoming royalty as some of them preferred to call themselves. This upcoming competition would fall on a separate weekend and last most of the weekend. It would take the best elements from the collegiate competition and take it to the next level.

Meanwhile, at the TriBoxalon festivities, the awards ceremony on Saturday night marked the end of the event. Or was it? What happened next took everyone present by surprise.

Buff walked over to Don, who was grabbing a drink at a table set up near the perimeter of the event space. "Hey, Don, mind if I talk to you for a minute?" he said in almost a whisper.

"Sure, Buff, I can always make time for you."

"Awesome. So here's the deal, I've got something I wanna say to Coco...up there," he said as he motioned to the stage. "In fact, it's something BIG. I've imagined it before, and while the scene is different, I want to make it happen for real this time...and I couldn't think of a better time to do it."

"I think I'm smelling what you're cooking," Don replied. "Say no more. I'll help you out."

"Thanks, man! That means a lot to me," Buff said, sounding relieved.

With that, the two parted ways. Don went onto the stage with a microphone, tapping it three times with his finger to ensure it was on. "Is everyone having a good time tonight?" he said loudly, trying to hype up the crowd. Everyone cheered and whistled, with some claps peppered in throughout the audience. "Great! Well, if you thought we were winding down, do I have a surprise for you. Buff, take it away!"

Don handed Buff the mic, who took it nervously. "Hey, Coco, could you please join me up here?"

A bit nervous and excited, Coco looked around her and saw people encouraging her to get up onto the stage. As she slowly sauntered down towards it, a flurry of thoughts ran through her head. "Was he going to actually ask *the* question? No...it couldn't be...or could it? This does seem like the perfect opportunity. Now, I hope he does because it would be a shame if he squandered such a great opportunity. I already know he is really into me, and he definitely knows I am into him." As she mused, she started having an increasingly growing grin on her face as she walked up the few steps between the ground and the top of the stage platform.

Buff grabbed Coco's hand, helping her up more in a chivalrous way than anything. She took his hand and got up onto the stage. The two of them stood in front of each other, both holding the other's hands within theirs. As Buff gazed into Coco's eyes, being mesmerized by their beauty, he nearly forgot what he was doing. A few seconds had passed before Coco brought him out of his daze.

"Uhh, Buff, you there, babe?"

Startled back to reality, he remembered what he was doing. "Oh, uhh, yeah! I must have gotten completely enraptured by your stunning beauty," he replied while Coco giggled. "So, there is something I wanted to ask you."

A few gasps permeated throughout the crowd.

"Coco, you have been the light of my life for a while now. You have motivated me to become the best version of myself. I have the absolute hots for you. There is nothing I feel like we can't do. I think we're the ultimate power couple. You are my north star. I could not see myself with anyone else but you. Since you entered my life, you've been the beacon of light guiding me through darkness, the muse behind my motivations, and the essence of joy that fills my days. This journey of self-improvement was not embarked upon alone but was a path we ventured down together, hand in hand, with our hearts leading the way. In this shared journey, I've found an undeniable truth: my world is infinitely brighter with you in it. My affection and desire for you are as boundless as the skies. In your eyes, I find the dreams I wish to chase, and in your smile, the home I've longed for. Together, I believe there is no summit we cannot reach, no storm we cannot weather, and no dream too distant to realize, which we have proven to be true today. So, I ask you now, as I bend my knee...will you marry me?

Everyone was utterly silent. There was no sound besides the low hum of the HVAC and other equipment.

"YES!"

The cheers throughout Tasty Lane were deafening. Buff got up and took Coco into his arms before kissing passionately. As their lips parted, they looked into each other's arms for a fondness and mutual feeling of being each others' *everything*.

After the rather spontaneous proposal and big awards night, everyone was in a jovial mood, as if they all received a contact high from the events that had just transpired. However, back in Level 1, Lucas and Coco had just unlocked a new level of awkwardness they didn't realize was possible. After all, the two had their own budding relationship emerging, albeit much slower than Buff Pepper and Coco Twain.

Back in Escape Control Central...

"Wow...didn't see that playing out the way it did..." Lucas expressed in disbelief.

"Yeah...quite a shocker. I mean, I figured they'd get engaged but, so soon?" Coco replied.

"Who knows...at this rate, they may be married by tomorrow!" "No way...could they?"

"Let's just say I wouldn't be surprised."

Coco and Lucas shared an awkward silence for a few moments before Lucas spoke.

"I think they make an excellent couple. And since they're based on us, I can see us—"

"Yes?!" Coco's eyes started sparkling, and her face began beaming. "I see us ending up just as happy as them...together."

Lucas did it. He finally said the quiet part out loud, subtly, and it felt fantastic to him. He got close to Coco and came in to bring her into an embrace...hugging her with his left arm while bringing his right hand up to caress the back of her head, bringing it closer to his. The inner fire of both of them was ignited, and they were breaking down the self-imposed barriers they had between them. Pretty soon, they would follow Buff and Coco down the same path of amorous felicity.

Steve and Y-Ali watched dumbfounded from their chairs before Steve spoke up.

"There it is! SO glad you two are no longer beating around the bush with this love affair you both want so much. And I fully support it. But let's just take a moment to bask in the success of the TriBoxalon down on Level 2. It's been a great Lucas Disney Production's success!"

Lucas snapped out of his romantic daze when he heard those three words.

"Hold the phone, Steve. I've got some concerns about that name. If we launch using 'Lucas Disney Enterprises,' there could end up being a messy legal battle with the big Disney!"

The group fell utterly silent.

"Wait...you're telling ME this? Aren't you the one who made that announcement on LinkedIn just the other day about your shell corp, which operates the equity investments that you're calling LUCAS DISNEY ENTERPRISES?! How is that any different?" Steve was utterly confused and a bit shocked.

"Yeah, Lucas! What gives?" Coco said. "I saw that LinkedIn announcement as well, and, to be honest, I got a little pissed off when I saw it. As you know, Steve and I are both heavily invested in BeTells, and I demand you change the name of the firm...and not only that, but I think you should cut us in as well."

"Alright, I can sense some tension, and I know I'm sending mixed signals, so let me explain. I thought it would be a fun idea to go with that name, and it really was. But today, I have been mulling over that idea. I know my LinkedIn says that, but I haven't had the time to update it. As you know, I've been holed up here a whole lot this week."

"So you agree it's a terrible idea?" Steve asked.

"Yes, terrible. Dreadful. Horrendous. I want to avoid us getting into any hot water, so I've nixed the idea." Lucas concluded his remarks on the matter while staring into Steve's eyes. Steve cocked his head, cradled his chin with the thumb and forefinger of his right hand, and broke his stare with Luke to look down at the floor. As Steve looked away, Coco reached out and grabbed two fingers from Lucas' left hand and told him, "I've always loved your middle name and you've always been my Elvis. Why don't you marry me and change your name to Elvis Oprahprada?"

Everyone is stunned except for Coco, who was beaming, with a face displaying fulfillment and a deep, conscious smile that gazed deeply into Lucas' eyes. The two embraced as before to seal the deal. Lucas then spoke out to her.

"Yes, we'll be married but I'll keep my name and change the name of our venture to Lucas Elvis Enterprises!'"

<u>GUIDING LIGHT MANTRA CHAPTER 9:</u>
The act of standing to deliver results to compete with others enables me to accept wisdom while exercising my mind, spirit, and body.

Chapter Ten

The Road to Authen City

"I keep cruisin."
(Taylor Swift from "Shake it Off")

As the dust settled on the unforgettable collegiate TriBoxalon, Lucas gathered his BeTells dream team for a debrief that quickly turned into a brainstorming session for the next big event. The room was filled with a mix of exhaustion and exhilaration, a testament to the whirlwind of success they'd just experienced.

"I think it's safe to say our collegiate TriBoxalon was a roaring success!" Lucas couldn't contain his enthusiasm, his words echoing off Escape Control Central's walls.

Coco, leaning back with a smirk that could set the room ablaze, added her own spicy twist to the conversation.

"I'll say! Buff Pepper and Coco Twain sure threw in that surprise at the end with that spontaneous proposal. Made me realize you and I need to make up for lost time," she said, her gaze locking with Lucas's in a moment charged with unspoken promises.

Lucas, momentarily flustered but ever the professional, redirected the focus. "I look forward to that, but business before pleasure. We've got to map out the TriBoxalon competition with the high school homecoming kings and queens from the LA and DFW areas."

Coco, always ready with a solution, chimed in. "Well, it shouldn't be too much work. We're pretty much following the collegiate template and adjusting it for high schoolers." Her confidence was infectious,

but Lucas's next point introduced a new layer of complexity to their planning.

"Yes, pretty much. The key requirement we will need to enforce is that everyone who competes is at least 18 years old. This wasn't an issue with the collegiate crowd, but some high school seniors are still 17, so let's ensure we have some minimal KYC done to confirm they're of-age," Lucas pointed out, his mind already racing through the logistics.

Don, ever the pragmatist, nodded in agreement. "I'm sure we can add that requirement to the application process," he said, his voice a steady anchor in the storm of ideas swirling around the room.

"Excellent," Lucas replied, his gaze sweeping across his team, each member brimming with the excitement of the challenge ahead. "So, as with the TriBoxalon we just had, we will source half of the homecoming royalty from DFW and half from LA. That split will ensure both regions are equally represented."

Initially, the meeting was a debrief and transformed into a lively planning session, with each member contributing their expertise and humor to the mix. The camaraderie within the team was palpable, their banter laced with the kind of wit and sarcasm that could only come from a group that had been through the trenches together.

Steve, who had been quietly taking notes, looked up with a sly grin. "So, are we going to have another surprise proposal at this one, or should I start planning the entertainment now?"

The room erupted in laughter, the tension of planning momentarily dissolved by Steve's jest. Catching his breath between laughs, Don added, "Let's just make sure it's not between any high schoolers. We don't need that kind of drama on our hands!"

"Also, what about recruiting, marketing, and all that?" Yolanda asked.

"Right. The key is that people first know about the high school TriBoxalon so that they can sign up. We've got our partners over at ViralSponsors.com, but we will also be doing our own marketing and promotion for targeted focus. We're going to need a strategic approach that focuses on engaging our target audience. The goal is to create buzz, see high participation rates from our marketing, and see these high schoolers being competitive while being observant of the competition's rules."

"Sounds good, but what's the strategy in that case?" Yolanda asked.

"It would have to be a multifaceted plan. First, we define our objectives and audience. Second, we develop the event framework. After that, we begin defining our recruitment strategy, marketing and promotion, and logistics and support."

"I'd say we've defined our objectives and audience already, right?" Coco asked.

"Yeah," Lucas replied. "We can also provide handy info to distribute to potential high school TriBoxalon competitors. In fact, we started doing that during the awards ceremony of the collegiate TriBoxalon, and we have been seeing the word get out pretty rapidly from that and onto social media. We're currently trending on social media, a key exposure platform for our target high school audience. We also have seen quite a lot of engagement."

"That's fire!" Y-Ali exclaimed. "That kind of organic grassroots marketing is the best kind because it's *authentic*, and authenticity is the currency of the new generation. That's why traditional marketing doesn't work that well on Gen Z. Even if influencers are getting paid to promote something, young people perceive them as more believable than some overly-sanitized ads."

"You've got a point there, Y-Ali," Lucas said while in a thinking stance, pondering. "I think we need to be where our target audience is, which in this case is high school seniors. I know that would be the platform to target, and not just relying on grassroots marketing, but also showing authentic content directly from thrivXR on there. You could even pay to get some authentic videos get more reach so that they get more exposure and go viral."

"That's a great idea, Y-Ali," Lucas said. "I'm not on social media much, but I know it gets the eyeballs, so we will make sure to place greater priority and emphasis on that being a primary way to reach high school seniors. And we could target that expanded reach based on the LA and DFW areas specifically, right?"

"Totally. You can micro-target and niche down as much as you want so that you get the most for your money," Y-Ali replied.

"Great input, Y-Ali," Lucas said. "We should also get our branding down. Most of what we used for the collegiate TriBoxalon should be used for the high school senior competition. However, what we could update is a slogan or tagline that resonates with high school seniors. Any ideas?"

"How about 'Leap into Legacy: Your Chance to Shine!'" asked Yolanda.

"Great stuff. Loving it," Lucas replied. "Any others to compare?"

"What about 'Graduate with Glory' as one?" asked Don. "Nice; short and punchy. Anyone else?"

The room was silent for a few moments as Lucas looked to see if there were any other ideas. It seems the team was thinking, but not much else was coming up to the surface.

"Alright, don't think too hard about it. This is something we can workshop later. Let's move to talking about testimonials and ambassadors," Lucas said. "I think we should reach out to Champions who participated in our most recent TriBoxalon to promote the upcoming one. This should inspire and increase participation when, like you said Y-Ali, we take the authenticity angle to heart and run all the way with it. People would love to get a firsthand account of the TriBoxalon. Who better than an unbiased source like one of the previous champions?"

"Great idea!" Don exclaimed. "I can get our staff to reach out to all of the competitors and get some testimonials."

"Perfect," Lucas replied. "And to pair with those, we have the ambassadors. Our chief ambassadors, I think, need no introduction– Buff Pepper and Coco Twain."

"Of course!" Steve proclaimed. Not only did they win the collegiate TriBoxalon, but they got friggin' *engaged* at the awards ceremony!"

"Couldn't be a better pick!" Coco said with excitement.

"I agree. Buff and Coco it is," Lucas returned. "We'll get them out on the circuit, performing interviews, speaking directly to our target audience in videos we post on social media, and other things we'll cook up. Those two are sure to surprise us even more than they already have, I'm sure."

"As part of our recruitment strategy, what about we directly engage with all of the high schools in DFW and LA so that we can work directly with the ones that end up delivering us the competitors? They could help us promote the event," Yolanda said.

"I like that," Lucas replied. "We could maybe involve presentations during school assemblies, have information sessions with sports teams, and other direct engagement activities."

"And highlight the benefits of participating, including the prizes, recognition, and other flexes," Y-Ali added.

"Sure, why not? We could add showcasing competitors and winners as part of our digital campaign," Lucas returned. "We could motivate the homecoming kings and queens in all sorts of ways aligned with us staying authentic while attracting stellar competitors."

"What about community engagement?" Yolanda asked. "Shouldn't we contact local media outlets and community organizations to help promote the event? Maybe get some extra logistical support and the like."

"Yes, I think engaging the community should be integrated into our overall strategy. We can target local businesses that are the kinds high school seniors frequent. That helps us maximize our positive impact with our campaign for the TriBoxalon."

"Anything we need to go over regarding the competition's framework that varies from the TriBoxalon we just had?" asked Yolanda.

"It's going to be very similar to the previous one, with the main distinction, of course, being the different pool of competitors. But since you bring it up, we will need to get the scheduling right. We should cross-reference any proposed dates for the TriBoxalon with school functions like exams, holidays, games, and all of that. Let's ensure we choose a date and time that minimizes conflicts with academic responsibilities and extracurricular activities."

"I'll task one of our staff to do that research," Don said.

"Great, that will ensure we have the best turnout we can, both with competitors and the audience," Lucas replied.

"What's our tech integration stack looking like, by the way?" Steve asked, always interested in that side of things more than anything.

"As you saw during the collegiate TriBoxalon, we had a lot of tech integration for making registration more efficient, live streaming and real-time updates during the event, and other things. We can add more as well if it is aligned with improving the quality and exposure of the competition."

"What about Max?" Steve said.

"What *about* Max? Lucas asked, wondering where he was going with this.

"Oh, I don't know...he's just about the most expensive piece of hardware thrivXR has, and as an incredibly advanced android with AGI and remarkable skin, I'd say he should be there at the TriBoxalon." Lucas and Coco exchanged awkward glances.

"Yeah...Max..." Lucas started saying under his breath. "What's that?" retorted Steve.

"Max kind of has a mind of his own, you know..." "So you don't think he'll show up?"

"No, no...I do. It's just that, him being a Level 3 character and all, I don't exactly have as much control over him as I did when I was poking and prodding him in his past life as a Tesla droid. I can use my telepathic superpowers to try and contact him from our reality to wherever he phases out, but I can't ever be certain he will do what I say. As AGI, he is pretty much an independent thinker...and turns out he's quite a smart 'guy' at that."

"True. We did make him really smart, didn't we? Funny to think how Max Poz started as an AI avatar on my computer. Now look at him– traveling between realities in ways we can't explain."

"Yep. All we can do is put out the call into the ether, and we hope he graces us with his presence. If he does end up making it to the TriBoxalon, which keep in mind, he didn't make it to the collegiate one, his presence may overshadow the competition itself. Imagine the worldwide press!" Lucas exclaimed.

"You're right. That would be like opening up Pandora's Box in front of eight billion people," Steve replied.

"Yeah. Let's just say if it's meant to be, it's meant to be. Who knows. Maybe Max is the secret ingredient for thrivXR and BeTells to become a global phenomenon, with hundreds of thrivXR locations!"

The entire room marinated in the idea. It was a massive dream and vision, but with Max looping around across multiple levels of creative reality, it seemed as if anything was possible. Lucas then shifted the conversation to the high school competition preparations.

"Oh, and before I forget, I know we said Buff and Coco will be our TriBoxalon ambassadors, but I don't think I mentioned that they will also be hosting the high school competition."

"Of course that makes sense!" Coco beamed. "Since Buff is from Dallas and Coco T is from LA, they could each recruit high school seniors from both first hand. There is no better couple than our Level 2s, right?"

Lucas laughed and agreed. "Can't say there is." We can incorporate popup events and equipment demos in both LA and Dallas and have Buff and Coco T showcase them. They'll be our ambassadors, reps, and hosts–the all-in-one package!"

"This is going great. I'm feeling really confident my investment is going to pay off...and I'm enjoying the process as well," Steve adds. "Planning the upcoming high school competition is great, but did we discuss preparing for the next season that will happen next year?"

"I don't think we did yet, but we could do that now since our core team is all present," Lucas replied.

"Perfect. So, as far as I remember, we mentioned off the cuff that there would be 13 different competitions. Is that still true?"

"Actually," Lucas answered. "We are planning to have 14 different comps next year, spread throughout 14 weekends. The split will be 50/50 for high school and college competitors, just like right now. We'll target seven weekends for the high school seniors and seven for the college crowd. And it won't necessarily be an open recruitment. We're going to focus our efforts on the time after Homecoming. The two people who will win the high school competition will host the first one next year."

"Makes sense to me," Yolanda said.

"Same," Y-Ali chimed in. "Just one question," she said as she raised her hand, "Are all the competitions happening here? I'm just thinking about the logistics of having people fly from LA over to Dallas for those competitions. That could be a barrier to entry."

"Great point, Y-Ali, and we've actually figured that part out," Lucas replied. What we are doing is that Buff and Coco T are going to be opening our LA brand of thrivXR! That's where the LA-side TriBoxalons will occur, making it a lot easier for people to compete and participate in them. We'll have half of all comps happening there."

There was a sudden rise in excitement and palpable joy at the idea of a thrivXR location in LA. After all, it was a prime location to target the cross-section of fitness influencers and actors.

"Great brainstorming sesh, everyone. I think we've unpacked a lot that we can neatly package afterward with the help of our extended team," Lucas told the group. "Thanks everyone for coming. I'm sure you're all excited about the upcoming competition, given just how successful the one we just had was."

"Totally stoked!" Steve exclaimed.

"Same. Alright, see you all next time. I'm going to put my head down and wireframe the second BeTells season that's going interstellar," Lucas said, giving Steve a clever wink.

As everyone left, Lucas stayed, sitting down to type away on his laptop what would become the scaffolding for a new BeTells season that would go in an entirely different direction than the first. It would be sci-fi, comedic, musical, and romantic. In other words...perfect.

It was a new day when Lucas, Coco, and Steve discussed The Road to Authen City, which they planned would define the second season of 13 episodes that would unveil Steve's vision of humanity inhabiting a planet located many galaxies away. They all sat down, Steve and Lucas laying out several pages of handwritten notes, as well as some typed-up material they were going to go over.

Just then, Coco arrived.

"Coco! What a pleasant surprise. Didn't think you'd be coming around today," Lucas said. "But it makes me really happy that you did."

Coco blushed. "Aw, thanks. I missed you too, Lucas," she said as she placed her hand over her heart.

"Lucas, you're not gonna believe this, but I learned something extraordinary...something paranormal through a buddy of mine," Steve said in a bit of a hushed tone. Lucas raised one eyebrow with building curiosity.

"Oh?"

"Yeah, a buddy of mine is head of the US Space Force research lab at MIT."

"You mean the Space Farce, right? Are they even doing anything of substance, or is it more like that show they made about it?"

"Oh, they are definitely doing real things there," Steve retorted. "This guy I'm telling you about has learned that a theoretical moss exists on a planet several galaxies away from Earth. The unofficial name they gave it is 'Ayedooper Fur' (pronounced "I do prefer") given its exceptionally furry nature. Apparently, it's like petting a chinchilla."

Coco's eyes pop, but nobody notices.

"Fascinating. And how exactly did they learn of the existence of this moss?" asks Lucas.

"That information was not divulged to me. Apparently, it involves some Cosmic Top Secret classified tech. In any case, they could go far beyond basic spectral readings and peer in through the planet's atmosphere to see the chemical compounds being released by life on the planet."

"It's amazing if true," Lucas said, still unconvinced but open to the possibility.

"I trust this guy, so I believe the info is sound. At least, I trust that he believes it to be true. In any case, that's not even the best part."

"Does this moss purr when it gets pet or something?" Lucas asked in jest.

"No, nothing like that," Steve said as he laughed. "Even better. This moss has remarkable curative, life restorative, and life extending properties...for humans!"

"Get out!"

"Seriously! They're already back-engineering the DNA profile they managed to put together simply from those chemical compounds they were picking up on that planet. I don't understand how, but biology isn't my forte. What they are apparently planning to do is recreate that moss right here on Earth!"

"That is so far out...and awesome! Imagine the benefits Ayedooper Fur could have for humanity. The implications are staggering."

"They sure are. And get this, Ayedooper Fur has converted raisins to grapes," Steve said.

"I dunno...I'm more of a grapes man, especially champagne grapes," Lucas replied, seemingly misunderstanding what Steve said.

"I'm glad you do, but I wasn't sharing my gastronomical persuasions, Lucas."

While Steve was having his discussion with Lucas, Y-Ali walked into the room and silently took a seat, noticing the two were intensely in a two-way conversation.

"I didn't say 'I do prefer raisins to grapes' but that Ayedooper Fur has converted raisins to grapes," Steve told Lucas. "It's like reversing dehydration. Imagine what it could do to shrivelly, old human skin– it could plump it right back up to how it looked when someone was in their 20s! Right after, Yolanda also made an entrance from a different door, sitting down next to Y-Ali without saying a word as well.

"Yo! Are you guys talking about the Road to Authen City?!" Y-Ali asked with barely contained excitement.

"We sure are," Lucas replied.

"Awesome! But I'm with Lucas on this one, except I thought you said that you're 'racing two grapes' instead of whatever you actually said," Y-Ali shared with a laugh.

"Ah, I guess it's pick on Steve day today, and I didn't get the memo," Steve returned sarcastically.

"We're just teasing," Lucas said with a chuckle.

"Wait, you guys are missing the plot...which I need to know involves me and where exactly I will be as far as my role goes," Yolanda interjected. She was fixated on what her role would end up being in the second season. "And Steve...I'm pretty sure you said you're 'raising two grapes,' so I don't know why you're that surprised."

"Alright, that's it!" Steve says with a shriek that has a tinge of desperation. The rest of the room laughed as they all teased him.

"I'm sure we could find the ideal role for you, Yolanda," Lucas replied. "I think it will help if you understand the story for the series a bit more."

"Do tell."

"Sure, so the Road to Authen City is going to bring to life the BeTells vision of inhabiting a planet in a nearby galaxy where it is prohibited to use vehicles on its surface. Only hovercrafts and hoverboards are allowed, as to now leave any negative impacts on the ground. Coco has developed this technology for electric bikes to cushion falls and eliminate accidents."

"That's environmentalism to the max, ain't it?" Yolanda said.

"That's the idea," Lucas returned. "This planet represents how starkly different Earth could be, and better, while still seeing the march of Progress move forward. Environmentalism doesn't have to mean we all become luddites and live like hunter-gatherers or something like that."

"Intriguing," returned Yolanda. "And what about this Ayedooper stuff?"

"Ayedooper *Fur*," Lucas corrected. "It's going to be an integral aspect of the series, based on something real that was discovered on a planet far, far…far away. In our series, it will be created using highly advanced technology that can take three oxygen molecules with a negative charge and have them stick together with a nebulous morphic field binder. The science of it is still being workshopped, but the focus will be on Ayedooper Fur being able to provide life- enhancing properties, especially when it comes to rejuvenation."

Coco stares directly into Lucas's eyes, "Ok, so I can share this with you because you have all opted into our confidentiality agreement. Based on my prior work with the human genome, I was approached, and subsequently, I've actually inked a joint venture with the Space Force to develop Ayedooper Fur from the microscopic photographic imaging into actuality using wet nanotechnology."

"So, maybe my character could take this stuff and be transformed to have a stunningly youthful glow, right?" Yolanda asked.

"Yep, we can do that. With the magic of AI and CGI today, we can do that without layers of makeup and other more uncomfortable avenues," Lucas told her.

"The Space Force determined this stuff does exist, and we're taking on the role of popularizing it in our series. What I am doing right now is mapping out the atmospheric properties of the planet way out there where this show would take place, along with the ground- level environment. It's a bit of world-building, which I really enjoy."

"That's why I leave those sorts of reality creation aspects to Steve. He is really passionate about creating entirely new worlds. Hey, Steve, maybe you could take up being a sci-fi writer," Lucas taunts him as he gives him an elbow nudge.

"That'd be great if I didn't suck at writing," he said as the room laughed.

"Since Coco, Y-Ali, and Yolanda are here now, I'd like to congratulate you. Season One of *Down at the Scene* has been so successful that it has propelled the fortunes of BeTells to the stratosphere. Along with that success has been the success of our Champions, who have all seen massive wealth generation that continues to grow.

The exponential explosion of prosperity and success seems to have been multiplied due to the IPO of the BeTells Creative Reality TV Agency to a level that is requiring a massive acquisition in order to maintain the valuation of our enterprise."

"A good problem to have!" shouted out Steve.

"It sure is," replied Lucas. "It requires us to expand what feels comfortable and normal as far as wealth generation goes. This ties into having an abundance mindset and avoiding upper-limiting, which people do way too often when they get to levels of wealth so great that it makes them uncomfortable. Knowing this, we can adjust our mindset to the point where we can literally feel that this new, profoundly and exponentially escalated level of wealth is completely normal and deserved."

"That's a great point. Mindset is key," Steve added. "It's why you see the majority of lotto winners lose it all within a few years. They became so uncomfortable with how much money they had that they didn't do the inner work necessary to keep that money and make it grow *while* also enjoying what that money can provide."

"Exactly," Lucas replied. "Thankfully, I think everyone on our team has a well-established success mindset where upper-limiting isn't much of an issue."

"Speaking of having a success mindset, I wanted to share something with you all here that's big...*really* big."

Everyone's ears perked up to hear what Steve had to say. "I am going to acquire Tesla and SpaceX."

Absolute silence permeated the room. "Come again?" asked Yolanda.

"That's right. I will go right up to Elon after securing a meeting with him and tell him point-blank that I'm buying him out."

"Your confidence is almost overwhelming, but I like it," Lucas replied. "May I ask one question though...*why?*"

"I know it may sound crazy, but hear me out. As you all probably know, Tesla and SpaceX have come under massive criticism and public outcry over concerns that the robots they're building have become too powerful. The last thing humanity needs on its hands is a robot rebellion. We know how that goes in the movies and shows."

"You got that right. OK, I think I see where you're going with this. You want to save humanity from having robot overlords," Lucas said tongue-in-cheek.

"In a way, yes. The solution I have come up with involves harnessing the technology developed for the droids and converting it into AI exoskeletons that require a human at the core. That way, a safeguard is in place so that the robots are not primed to become autonomous killbots."

"That's a genius idea, Steve! Really. Since the march of Progress cannot be stopped, what we can do is make sure it has some wisdom guiding it with safeguards in place like the one you have in mind," Lucas told him.

"Thanks." Steve slowly and thoughtfully intones, "Yeah, I think with me at the helm, instead of that other guy, we can get legislation pushed worldwide that would require that all AI robots be retrofitted as exoskeletons that derive their focus and direction entirely from human impulse direction. I am confident BeTells will be able to get the approval from the FTC to complete the acquisition and help bring my vision into reality."

"It's a great plan...but where does that leave our friend Max?" asked Yolanda. There was an awkward silence in the room. Lucas was the first to speak up after a few moments.

"Yeah, Steve, what *about* Max?" asked Lucas.

"I've thought about that, and I'm the one who helped you and Coco with bringing him to 3D life, which I initially didn't anticipate. But what we could do is retrofit Max as well. Sure, it may take some adjustments, and he won't be the same as he is now, but if we want to safeguard humanity, the rule will have to be universal."

The room had a sad vibe at the thought of Max no longer being the same Max they have all come to know and love. However, they knew it was for the best.

"I'm gonna miss that guy," Don said, choking up.

"Oh, come on, Don, he's not dying or anything. He's just getting an exoskeleton upgrade, so someone like you or me can hop in and take over the controls if need be," Lucas said, trying to reassure him.

"Ah, alright. In that case, I think it will be fine, and I won't get so worked up about it," Don replied.

The gang continued brainstorming and planning the high school TriBoxalon competition. Given the groundwork already being done for the collegiate competition, there wasn't much to do except make a few adjustments and some improvements where lessons were learned. The BeTells team continued to hash out and finalize the details. They were ready to take thrivXR and BeTells to the next level, and the TriBoxalon was a surefire way to get the exposure needed to do that.

Meanwhile, Buff Pepper and Coco Twain were going to have a *very* special day coming up.

"Let's get married, Coco!" Buff said excitedly. After just proposing to Coco Twain recently at the TriBoxalon awards ceremony, he had no desire to wait the standard year or however long was socially expected.

"Married? But Buff, you just proposed to me!"

"I know, babe, but I'm crazy about you. I already know I want to spend the rest of my life with you. There is nobody better than you in this entire world. You're my *forever*."

"Aw, Buff, you are such a romantic. OK...then I say...LET'S GET MARRIED!" Coco threw her arms around Buff and kissed him while letting one foot lift behind her.

"We're going to have an amazing wedding, Coco. I know this is all spontaneous, but I'm the type of guy that goes where the energy is, and right now, the energy is rushing through my entire body and telling me to do this."

"I love how in tune you are with your emotions. You're the perfect man," Coco T told him lovingly.

"I know...let's have next week! We can make it a small, intimate affair with just close friends and family and then have an absolutely epic wedding after the awards ceremony for the upcoming TriBoxalon!"

"That's perfection! I love it," exclaimed Coco. "It's so romantic to have a wedding in a way similar to how you proposed to me in the first place! Gosh, can I love you any more than I already do?"

"I'm glad you love the idea, babe," Buff replied.

Buff and Coco brought together their closest friends and relatives and had their wedding officiated by a wedding officiant who Buff knew through a friend of a friend to make it as comfortable and cozy of a scene as possible. He wanted to save the theatrics for the wedding, which he already started planning something that would absolutely dazzle and amaze Coco.

As if a sign that they were destined to be together, the setting sun cast a splendid backdrop that seamlessly blended the marvels of nature with the couple's celebration of love and unity. As the sun dipped below the horizon, it painted the sky in hues of orange, pink, and purple, while an unexpected rain shower earlier in the day alchemized the sky by displaying a breathtaking double rainbow arching over their union. This doubleshot of a natural wonder seemed to encapsulate the essence of the occasion — a vibrant and beautiful beginning of a new chapter.

As he looked up at the natural marvel, Buff felt an overwhelming sense of gratitude and awe. The sight of the rainbow and the stunning cloud sunset seemed to him a good omen, a celestial approval of their union. It reflected his internal state — a mix of excitement for the future and a deep, resonant joy.

Buff looked at Coco, thinking how fortunate he was to begin their shared journey under such a magnificent sky, believing it to be a metaphor for their life ahead, filled with both light and color after any storm.

For Coco, the moment was absolutely ethereal. The double rainbow and the dramatic sky seemed dreamlike. She felt as if the universe itself was celebrating their love, wrapping them in a canvas of spectacular beauty. The scene mirrored her emotions — vibrant, hopeful, and full of promise. It reinforced her belief in new beginnings and the beauty that follows after overcoming challenges together.

Among the guests was an elderly aunt who was moved by what she was seeing. To her, the rainbow was a symbol of hope and renewal. She had witnessed many sunsets and many beginnings in her day, but this one, with the obviously joyous occasion it accompanied, reminded her of the enduring beauty of life and the importance of cherishing each moment and making it count. The sight inspired her to reflect on her own life experiences, recognizing that after every hardship she had faced, she had always survived and even thrived– the pinnacle of a self-actualized life.

The wedding planner, often behind the scenes and focused on the details of event execution, took a rare moment to pause and absorb the beauty before her. While she was usually focused on orchestrating perfection, she found the evening's natural display humbling. It was a touching reminder that some of the most beautiful moments cannot be planned or predicted.

Against the backdrop of Buff and Coco T's wedding, this sunset and rainbow inspired her because she recognized the magic this beautiful world has to offer to elevate and enhance human experiences to a transcendental plane.

After the wedding and their much-anticipated honeymoon to Tahiti, the two love birds were back in Dallas, eager to prepare for their mock wedding.

"I know we just got back from Tahiti, but I gotta tell you, I'm really itching to start planning our mock wedding at the TriBoxalon awards ceremony," Buff told Coco T.

"Let's do it to it!" exclaimed Coco.

"It's not a lot of time between now and then, but I can call in a few favors some people owe me so that it's going to be really special. I've already got ideas spinning in my head. I don't want to give anything away, but don't be surprised if I pop the question again, but this time, do it with such fanfare and gravitas. I just know I'm going to sweep you right off your feet."

"Oh, Buff, you don't have to! I'd live in a shoe with you…but I'm also not going to stop you. I am SO excited to see what surprise you've got planned," she said excitedly.

One week later, Buff and Coco have the most important day of their lives. It would become the day they would seal their lifelong commitments to one another with a kiss…and an epic party.

The scene was Tasty Lane, right next door to the thrivXR Fitness Studio, where the high school TriBoxalon competition was happening. Don Everyday, GM of thrivXR, was the MC once again.

There was a lot of fanfare and buzz in the crowd this evening–triple the crowd of the collegiate TriBoxalon. Attendees were swaying to the rhythm of the music pumping through speakers set up around the stage, with some feeling compelled to dance when a banger would come on every now and then. Some people even brought their children, who were running around the scene, playing and laughing. Even a dog was walking by the scene, sniffing at some people who were holding hors d'oeuvres. The lively and diverse crowd made it apparent that the BeTells marketing strategy had worked.

Music was pumping through speakers throughout the scene as Don did a light jog up the stage stairs to give an announcement.

"Can I have everybody's attention, please!"

"What's he doing?" Lucas wondered. "He already announced the competition's winners."

"I know we already know who our winners are, announced by our hosts of this competition who were the winners last year, Buff and Coco. However, there's something really special someone wants to say and do here tonight. Are you ready for an epic surprise?!"

The throngs of people in the audience cheered and whistled at the top of their lungs.

"Buff, Coco…could you two please come up here?" Don said to both of them.

"Uh oh…what's happening?" Coco said to Lucas, feeling increasingly awkward as to what was possibly about to happen. The feelings that Lucas and Coco had for one another, while taking a step towards becoming stronger, were still not at the level that Buff and Coco's seemed to be…but they were clearly inching their way in that direction.

Buff and Coco got up onto the stage, and Buff took the mic Don handed him.

"Thank you, Don, and thank you to all you amazing people tonight!" Buff shouted out to the crowd, eliciting a flurry of cheers. I wanted to say something to Coco, if none of you mind."

The crowd let out a subtle laugh before Buff continued. Coco had a twinkle in her eye and a smile on her face.

"You may remember that last year, this is the event I proposed to Coco, right here where I'm standing. It was a spur-of-the-moment sort of decision on my part, and while Coco and the crowd loved it, I decided to do some planning behind the scenes for a redo of that proposal in a BIG way."

Coco was caught by surprise. What did Buff have in store?

Buff looked over to Don, signaling him with his hand, pointing to give him the all-clear to do what came next. There was a massive projector screen behind them on the stage, towering over everyone standing there. The air buzzed with anticipation as an advanced AR projector, a marvel of modern technology, came to life. It illuminated the scene with a dazzling array of light and color, transforming Tasty Lanc into a real-life fantasia.

Projections included sprawling digital landscapes, each designed to inspire the audience–and Coco. There were astronomical wonders like planets, constellations, and nebulas, all up close and personal, unlike the crowd had ever experienced. Meteor showers, comets, and the aurora borealis were also on grand display.

An interactive light show started as well, where the attendees' movements were tracked and reflected in the projections, creating a dynamic and interactive visual experience that blew everyone's mind. Coco started jumping up and down with joy and clapping her hands, all of which the AR projector responded to with waves of color that moved with her and with virtual fireworks exploding in response to her movements.

As the outstanding demonstration concluded, the crowd erupted in thunderous applause...not just for Buff and Coco, but for the vision of a future where technology could elevate and enhance 3D reality to create a more engaging, personalized, and immersive experience. The projector faded, leaving behind a sense of wonder and excitement for what might come next.

"I can see you all enjoyed that!" Buff shouted out to the crowd. "But I'm not done. Coco, there's something special just for you I've planned."

Buff pointed once more to Don, who spoke into the ear of someone else beside the stage who looked like a technician of some sort. After a few moments, a sudden hush fell over the scene even while the crowd was still basking in the afterglow of the AR projection display. All of the lights at the outdoor area of Tasty Lane dimmed, directing everyone's gaze upward to the night sky. It would now become the canvas for the evening's most breathtaking spectacle yet.

Without warning, the air filled with the soft hum of drones...over one hundred, emerging like stars against the night's canvas. They took their places one by one, with their movements precise and choreographed with an elegance that emphasized the technology controlling them. Buff, Coco, and the crowd watched in awe, their anticipation building as the drones began to form letters against the backdrop of the night sky, illuminated by the drones' lights.

W...I...L...L

The formation continued, with it becoming quickly apparent that each letter would be a testament to Buff's unwavering commitment and love for Coco. Now in on the surprise, the crowd watched with bated breath as the message took shape.

Y...O...U M...A...R...R...Y M...E...?

The question hung in the air, spelled out in brilliant lights, a high-tech declaration of love that bridged the gap between technology and tradition. Coco T, caught completely by surprise, turned to Buff, her eyes wide with amazement, love, and joy. The crowd's silence was palpable, but they already had a good idea of what she would say, given the widely-issued coverage of Buff's proposal at the previous TriBoxalon.

With a smile that lit up her face brighter than the drone display above, Coco turned to the audience, then back to Buff, and yelled with all the happiness in her heart, "YES!"

The crowd erupted into cheers and applause, a symphony of joy matching the dazzling sky display. Buff took Coco into his arms, and as they embraced, the drones began a new dance, weaving intricate patterns and shapes in celebration, creating a spectacle of light and motion that mirrored the joy of the moment.

The drone show, orchestrated by Buff as a surprise within a surprise, became the highlight of the evening and left a big impression on all who witnessed it. It was a proposal that transcended the ordinary, leveraging the magic of the moment to celebrate love in a way that was as unique and memorable as Buff and Coco's journey together.

Lucas and Coco had to pick up their jaws off the floor after what they just saw.

"He proposed AGAIN?! And with such fanfare!" Coco exclaimed. "How romantic is that!"

Lucas, feeling as awkward as he could possibly feel and a bit embarrassed at how good Buff was at being romantic, made a snide remark. "Yeah, well, he's being a bit flashy, isn't he?"

Coco got slightly irritated for a moment before she softened as she realized Lucas was jealous of how well Buff pulled off the proposal. "Sure, it's a lot, but just look at Coco T's face. She's absolutely over the moon. Maybe take some pointers from Buff over there," she said with a wink and a smile.

GUIDING LIGHT MANTRA CHAPTER 10:

Connecting in emotionally committed relationships enables me to access the best that humanity has to offer.

Chapter Eleven

Down at the Scene

"Now we're here."
(from Drake's "Started from the Bottom")

It was time for the high school TriBoxalon. An overflowing group of Champions, who were Homecoming Kings and Queens from DFW and LA high schools, buzzed, bantered and bathed in mutual excitement at the entrance into the hi- octane competition.

Blending physical prowess with eXtended Reality attracted a diverse crowd of young competitors, each with their own distinct aspirations and internal narratives. Among them was Maja.

Joining the TriBoxalon from Los Angeles, Maja was a first-timer in Dallas. She had also never even heard of XR fitness equipment prior to being contacted to participate in the competition, yet she was incredibly excited. She was a girl who balanced her academic pursuits with a keen interest in technology and working out, which is why she saw the competition as the perfect amalgamation of her passions.

Small and seemingly agile, with an intensity in her eyes that reflected her focused and methodical approach to life, Maja paired all of this with practical attire. Yet, she also adorned herself with wearable tech gadgets to track her fitness metrics. Naturally, she asked for a Chain, because she was a go-getter unlike any other there that day. She would oscillate between confidence in her abilities and the pressure to excel academically. It was quite a pressure cooker life she lived. However, it was a catalyst for her to ponder about how technology could enhance and improve human performance. It was a big reason she agreed to make the trip to this boutique fitness studio in Dallas.

Maja had a relentless pursuit of excellence and a deep-seated desire to break stereotypes about women in STEM. She is a girl who is driven by the challenges she faces, using them as fuel to propel herself forward. It would be fitting that she found herself attracted to Ethan's laidback confidence and his natural athleticism–seeing in him a balance she strives to achieve herself.

Ethan was eyeing Maja, with a soft smile emerging as he saw her staring back at him. Coming from a small town in the Dallas-Fort Worth area, he came from quite a starkly different background than Maja. He grew up playing football and was the star quarterback in his senior year, which meant it was no surprise he was the Homecoming King for his high school. He viewed the TriBoxalon as an opportunity to expand his horizons and combine athleticism with XR...something he didn't know much about.

Tall and broad-shouldered, Ethan had a natural athletic build complemented by a disarming smile. His style was unassumingly casual, with a preference for comfort over trendiness, hence his sweatpants and muscle tank. He carried an air of easy-going confidence, tempered by moments of introspection as he contemplated his future beyond high school. Ethan was drawn to Maja's intensity and focus, admiring her dedication to being a winner at this TriBoxalon. While she opted for a Chain, Ethan leaned towards getting a Bracelet.

Close to the back of the line, with no rush in her demeanor to get inside, Isabel was one of the more artsy competitors at the TriBoxalon that day. Back home in LA, she was known for her creative projects that blended digital art with interactive elements.

The XR competition represented a novel challenge for her, offering a way to combine her artistic vision with physical activity.

Isabel stood out with vibrant pink hair and handmade accessories. Her poise was graceful, hinting at a hidden athleticism beneath her creative exterior. As a dreamer, she was often lost in her thoughts. She viewed the world through a lens of potential creations, seeing the TriBoxalon as another canvas for her imagination. She was driven by the need to express herself and to connect with others through her creations.

As she was casually sauntering into thrivXR, Isabel was captivated by Noah's analytical mind and his subtle artistic sensibilities, recognizing in him a kindred spirit who shared her appreciation for blending technology with creativity.

Standing right before Isabel, Noah was a bit of a math whiz, or "mathlete" as he jokingly referred to himself, an aspiring engineer from Dallas with a penchant for solving complex problems and a curiosity about the mechanics behind XR technology. He sees the TriBoxalon as a way to test his theoretical knowledge in a practical, competitive setting. Noah had a slight, unassuming frame with sharp, attentive eyes that missed nothing. His attire was simple, as he preferred utility over fashion, with the occasional science or math-themed t-shirt, which he decided against wearing to the TriBoxalon.

Noah was introspective, often caught up in his thoughts about future technologies and their implications. He struggled with social interactions but found comfort in the structured environment of competitions, which is why he wanted to participate in the TriBoxalon. A thirst for knowledge and a fascination with the potential of technology to solve real-world problems. Noah was driven by his intellectual curiosity and a desire to apply his skills in meaningful ways. Lucas definitely admired Isabel's creative mind, as well as her looks and her ability to see beauty in complexity, seeing her as someone who could understand and appreciate his unconventional interests.

Standing on the precipice of adulthood, these high school seniors were brought together by their shared interest in the TriBoxalon and BeTells, each bringing their unique perspectives, talents, and insecurities. Their interactions, both competitive and personal, reveal their depth, as well as the diversity of their motivations. Through the lens of this futuristic competition, they explored the limits of their physical and mental capabilities and the complexities of human connection, ambition, and the search for identity in a rapidly evolving world.

LATER THAT DAY...

Buff, a towering man of strength, and Coco, a vision of grace and power, stood hand in hand, gazing into each other's eyes. Don, the evening's master of ceremonies, stepped forward and started speaking.

"Oh my god, it's happening now?!" Coco yelled out with shock and surprise.

"Wow...I guess so!" Lucas added, also stunned and feeling a bit awkward.

"Tonight, beyond announcing the winners of the high school TriBoxalon competition, we also witness a spectacle of love and commitment. Yes, you've heard me right—a wedding!" Don started off saying, taking on the appearance of an unconventional officiant given the black muscle tank he was wearing.

"Buff and Coco have already embarked on their journey as husband and wife. Tonight, they've chosen to share their joy in a mock wedding, a testament to their love and partnership, in front of you, their extended family of supporters and friends."

A collective gasp, followed by a warm outpouring of applause, filled the room. Buff and Coco exchanged a knowing smile, their love becoming a tangible force.

Don continued, "Buff, do you take Coco to be your lawfully wedded wife, *again*, in sickness and in health, on gym days and rest days, for as long as you both shall live?"

Looking deeply into Coco's eyes, Buff delivered his vows with sincerity that hushed the room. "I do. Coco, in the gym of life, you are my ultimate spotter, ensuring I never falter. Together, we've tackled every challenge, turning setbacks into comebacks. I vow to be your partner in every workout and every walk of life, forever."

"And do you, Coco, take Buff to be your lawfully wedded husband?" Don asked. A tear glistened in Coco's eye as she responded to Don's question with equal passion.

"I do. Buff, standing by your side, I've found strength I never knew I had and a love that transcends all. You inspire me to be better in fitness and in life. I pledge to stand by you, to dream with you, and to build a future filled with love and laughter for all the days of my life."

The room, already teetering on the edge of emotional overflow, erupted into cheers as Don, with a flourish worthy of a Broadway finale, declared, "By the power vested in me by the state of celebration and joy, I now pronounce you, once again, husband and wife. Seal this moment with a kiss."

As Buff and Coco sealed their vows (again) with a kiss, the crowd stood, with their applause being thunderous, as they were celebrating not just the union of two souls but the spirit of love, commitment, and achievement they embodied.

This mock wedding, set against the backdrop of their recent TriBoxalon victory, was more than just a spectacle; it was a declaration of their journey together, a partnership built on mutual respect, unwavering support, and an unbreakable bond. Don wrapped his arm around his girlfriend Delilah as she rested her head on his shoulder. They took in the wonderful events that transpired that weekend and were satisfied with a job well done.

Meanwhile, Lucas and Coco were completely blindsided, feeling a complex array of emotions. They had known each other for years, yet their hearts had danced around the truth of their feelings. Today, something in the air seemed to spark a different kind of courage in them. Buff and Coco...it was definitely Buff and Coco. Lucas glanced at Coco, taking in her radiant smile and how her eyes shimmered with emotion. He cleared his throat, a nervous habit around Coco he had yet to shake off.

"You know, Coco, seeing them out there, it's like looking into a mirror, isn't it?"

Coco turned to him with a thoughtful expression. "If the mirror reflects two people ridiculously in love but too stubborn to admit it, then yes, absolutely."

Lucas laughed. Soft music started playing mysteriously in the background. "Exactly. I mean, we've been dancing around this for how long? Too long. I've seen you conquer the world...one role, invention, and investment at a time, and you've been there, cheering me on as I turned a wild dream about a boutique fitness studio and creative reality TV agency into reality."

Coco's laughter joined his, light and genuine. "Well, I do enjoy the perks of being a part of BeTells and thrivXR. Free membership? Is that how you reel them in?"

"Hey, I had to keep my favorite investor happy," Lucas retorted, his gaze softening. "But honestly, Coco, that's just it. I wanted you close because I couldn't imagine you not being a part of my life, professionally or... personally."

The energy between them shifted, charged with the weight of unspoken words finally making their way to the surface. Coco reached out, her hand finding his.

"Lucas, I've invested in a lot of things, but what I truly wanted to invest in was us. I just never knew how to say it."

Lucas took a deep breath, his decision made. He dropped to one knee, right there amidst the soft rustle of their surroundings, the laughter and chatter of the wedding a distant backdrop to their moment. He took Coco's hand in his, his heart racing.

"Coco, I don't want to spend another day pretending I don't know what this is between us. I love you. I love your brilliance, your passion, and the way we laugh together. Will you marry me and make me the happiest man alive?"

Coco's response was a mix of laughter and tears, the emotional cocktail of a moment too big and too beautiful. "Lucas, you had me at 'free membership.' *Of course*, I will marry you!"

As they embraced and kissed, the world around them seemed to pause, a perfect bubble of joy amid the ongoing celebration. Lucas whispered in her ear, "Just so you know, marrying me doesn't get you out of your annual membership renewal."

Coco pulled back, feigning shock. "What? That's outrageous! I demand a lifetime membership."

Lucas's laughter rang out, pure and happy. "For you, anything."

Their moment of lightheartedness and profound commitment was a testament to their journey—a mix of love, laughter, and the shared dreams of two hearts finally united. They were done beating around the bush. Lucas and Coco had finally begun their journey towards tying the knot.

A few months after their heartfelt proposal, Lucas and Coco's wedding day arrived, set against the picturesque backdrop of a nearby posh country club. The choice of venue was perfect, allowing their friends, family, and the teams from BeTells and ThrivXR—the fitness studio's staff and close associates—to join in the celebration with ease. The air was buzzy with excitement, a testament to the love and admiration everyone had for these two.

None other than Max Pozel was there...somehow reversing the loop and making his way into Level 1 reality. Not only would it be a surprise to Lucas, Coco, and everyone for that matter, but he would also divulge something quite shocking.

"Hey, Lucas; hey there, Coco!" he said.

"...MAX?!" Lucas exclaimed. "How in the he–oh, never mind. You go on and keep your secrets. But what are you doing here?"

"Isn't it obvious? I'm the guy who's marrying the two of you!"

Both Lucas and Coco were speechless. How could Max, an android, albeit looking more like a perfected human, officiate a wedding?

Aren't there laws against robots doing that sort of thing? They were experiencing a real mindbender.

"I see you're wondering how I could be your officiant and where the guy you hired went," Max said. "Simple. I became an ordained minister online this morning. The internet truly has everything, doesn't it?" he said with a grin. "Oh, and I made a deal with the original officiant. I slipped him $100 since I saw that done in a movie recently, and it seems humans do that if they want something to get done, but that normally wouldn't necessarily happen."

"Max, that's not a habit I would like to see you repeating that much." Coco said. "But it's sweet of you to want to officiate our wedding, so we happily accept, don't we, Lucas?" she said while elbowing Lucas in the ribs.

"Yes! Of course. We'll be delighted to have you as our officiant."

"Awesome! Thanks for giving me the OK. Hope I wasn't too forward, assuming you'd be fine with it."

"I couldn't think of anyone more fitting to marry us," Lucas told him.

The ceremony was set to begin, and as Lucas and Coco stood facing each other in front of all the attendees, the world around them seemed to fade away, leaving only the two of them in their shared bubble of love and anticipation. The setting sun cast a dreamy glow over the scene, enhancing the magical atmosphere.

Lucas, looking into Coco's eyes, began his vows.

"Coco, from the moment you walked into my life, you've been a force of nature, challenging, inspiring, and helping me in ways I didn't even know were possible. You've been my professional, my

muse, and my best friend. I promise to cherish you, to laugh with you, and to support you...to be your anchor in the storm and your companion in the sun. From this day forward, I vow to be yours in all things."

Coco, her eyes shimmering with tears and joy, took Lucas's hands in hers.

"Lucas, you are my heart's true companion, the one who sees me for who I truly am and loves me all the more for it. You've given me a home in your heart, a place where I belong. I promise to stand by you, to dream with you...to *thrive* with you, and to build a life with you filled with love, laughter, and endless adventure. You are my everything, and I vow to be yours until the end of time."

Their vows hung in the air, a sacred promise witnessed by their friends, family, staff, and team. The moment was surreal, a dreamlike culmination of years of friendship that had blossomed into a love deep and true.

Now tasked with sealing their union, Max couldn't resist adding his flair to the moment.

"By the power vested in me by the internet and by the love we all witness here today, I now pronounce you husband and wife. You may kiss."

As Lucas and Coco shared their first kiss as a married couple, cheers and applause erupted around them. The celebration was more than just a wedding; it was a testament to the journey of two people who had found each other, their souls intertwined in a love story that had only just begun. They would surely go on to accomplish tremendous feats together as a true power couple.

The evening continued with laughter, dancing, and joy, a reflection of Lucas and Coco's journey—a journey that had transformed from a friendship into a love that would last a lifetime.

At the front of the wedding reception, beside Lucas, Buff laughed, "And I always thought 'Never the Twain shall meet!' But now I must pronounce you Man & Wife."

"You know me, Coco, I always wanted to imprint the zeitgeist," bellowed Lucas with a wry smile as he addressed Coco all the way across the stunned and elated crowd.

A new chapter had begun in their lives, and it would end up being the most spectacular, transformational, and successful one yet. Their story was not over. No, it had just begun.

SIX MONTHS LATER...

"Yeah, so when I saw that the volume on my radio goes to 11, just like in *Spinal Tap*, I knew I had to buy the company," gloated Steve.

"OK, Steve, this will be the last chapter," agreed Lucas with a chuckle.

On a boat at an upscale resort in Lake Tahoe, Steve Yabbs and Elon Musk were seated, fishing poles locked into holsters so no need to hold them. The tension was laid on thick, as this was no simple get-together of two friends. No, this was business and the cutthroat kind. Steve knew how Elon operated and needed to bring his A-game to the table. While tensions were high, there was also an undercurrent of the absurd that only these two could bring to a negotiation of this magnitude.

With the calm demeanor of the seasoned tech mogul that he was, Steve leaned in, locking eyes with Elon.

"Elon," he began, his voice steady, "I've been thinking about the future of AI and robots. I believe that by combining our efforts, we can accelerate humanity's progress away from a dystopian future and towards one where humans will always call the shots. We don't need to have a potential robot uprising on top of the meta-crisis humanity's dealing with. That's why I want to buy Tesla and SpaceX."

Elon, unfazed, took a sip of his drink and displayed a spark of mischief in his eyes. He set his glass down and leaned back, a smirk playing on his lips.

"What? You're buying me out?" He shook his head, chuckling. "No, no, Steve. You've got it all wrong. I'm buying *you* out."

Steve raised an eyebrow, a slight smile tugging at his lips, recognizing the audacity only Elon could muster.

After regaining his composure, Steve chuckles, "For such an accomplished genius, I think your biggest legacy to humanity may be a lesson in humility."

Curious, with a furrowed brow, Elon wonders aloud, "Why do you say that?"

"Well, its become apparent that such an accomplished genius can still choose to act like an idiot!" laughs Steve.

Elon counters with his eyebrows raised, "Yeah well Steve, to be fair, Bill Browder warned us what can happen in his book RED NOTICE."

"Yeah, well, no matter what your motivation has been, we BeTells got the imagination and talent for sure, but Elon, with all due respect, I came here to offer you a chance to be part of history...to merge our dreams into a reality that will shape the future for the better, and safeguard it. And you think you're buying me out?" he said with a laugh.

Elon leaned forward, the light catching the edge of his determined expression. "Steve, my friend, it's not enough to dream in this world. You have to dream bigger. I'm not just looking to shape the future; I'm aiming to own it. How about this? Instead of buying each other out, we create a new company. We'll call it SpaceX-Tesla-Apple- Galaxy. STAG, for short. It's bold, it's innovative, it's... confusing, but think of the logo!"

Steve, momentarily taken aback by the audacity of the idea, couldn't help but let out a nervous laugh.

"STAG? That sounds like a bachelor party in space," Steve replied. "Besides, you're missing the whole point of why I called this meeting. I believe you are being careless with AI and robots. Didn't you say a couple of years ago that 'if you can't beat 'em, join 'em?' I firmly believe there need to be some major safeguards in place for your Tesla droids, and all robots with AGI for that matter. That's why I am here to make you an offer you can't refuse."

"Oh, really?"

"Yes," Steve said. "I'll be retrofitting all the Tesla droids with exoskeletons where humans are operating them instead of the robots being fully autonomous. I'm surprised you're not considering a guardrail like that, but I am, and I have the backing to buy you out, so let's cut a deal."

Elon, momentarily taken aback by the sheer boldness of Steve's idea, burst into laughter. "Steve, that's... that's utterly ridiculous! And completely brilliant. Humans in robot suits? It's like every sci-fi movie ever come to life. But why would you need to buy me out for that?"

"Because," Steve said, leaning back with a confident smile, "I believe that with my direction utilizing Ayedooper Fur, I can take this concept and truly make it a reality. There will be a new era of human empowerment. And don't worry, even though I don't think you will win and I wouldn't vote for you, as discussed, I'll back channel broker the deal on the US Senate floor for you to assume the nomination for POTUS...."

Elon smiled broadly, his eyes narrowing until he laughed heartily...

Steve actually heralds in a new age when he explains to Elon, "We have successfully replicated Ayedooper Fur, which is the manna from heaven with ultimate curative properties that provide quench for the human condition being the elemental oil to anoint for the elimination of disease, life extension and resonant goodness. Ayedooper Fur is essentially the material expression of profound, penultimate goodness and positivity. When injected into an exoskeleton, each and every negative impulse is decomposed and recombined as an energy source for the exoskeleton. Most astoundingly, when Ayedooper Fur interlocks with artificial intelligence, only goodness surges and replicates throughout, enabling massive replication strength for the essential goodness of the human spirit."

"International governments will rapidly enact legislation to piggyback on antinuclear proliferation treaties to eliminate both AI droids and nuclear weapons worldwide."

"Most effective though, humans will naturally deactivate with Ayedooper Fur exoskeletons and convert any and all ai droids to exoskeletons with Ayedooper Fur surging throughout. That will be the real gamechanger."

"So, humanity, empowered by and equipped with Ayedooper Fur exoskeletons will enter what will become known as the Age of Replication where elaborate, sophisticated exoskeletons will be created using wet nanotechnology which will, in turn, enable massive public work projects for goodness."

"That's really great, Steve. Uh, how can I help?" Elon wonders aloud.

He extended his hand across the table. "Alright, Steve. You've got yourself a deal. But, if you're doing this, I have a few stipulations for accepting your offer. I want these exoskeletons to be able to fly. And they should have a 'Mars mode'—just in case."

Steve thought about it momentarily, then shook Elon's hand.

"Deal, Elon. But I'm putting you in charge of the Mars mode. After all, who better to lead that than the man who's determined to die on Mars—just preferably not on impact."

Once the agreement was reached, the two visionaries sat back on the fishing boat, their conversation turning from negotiations to the wild possibilities of the future of emerging technologies like AI, XR, and others.

After that weekend ended, Steve flew back to Dallas, giddy with excitement to see the look on Lucas' face when he informed him of the remarkable news. Once he arrived, he quickly rushed over to the thrivXR Sports + Fitness studio, where Lucas was overseeing the installation of new XR equipment that had been delivered earlier that day. thrivXR had started expanding, with the Los Angeles location already picked out and building about to commence. To celebrate the eventual inauguration, Lucas would unveil a new kind of XR fitness experience unlike any other available up to that point.

Steve tapped Lucas on the shoulder. "Hey, Lucas, guess who's back with incredible news."

"Oh, I like this game," Lucas said without turning around. "A lucky leprechaun who is somehow tall enough to reach my shoulder."

"Close enough. It's me, Steve."

"I sensed you from the parking lot. Something's got you really excited from the looks of it," Lucas said after he turned around to face Steve.

"Four words–I bought out Elon."

In disbelief, Lucas exclaims "...what!!???"

"Oh, yeah. I actually got him to agree. I gave him an offer he couldn't refuse, ya know?" Steve said with a bit of flair.

"What's the deal?"

"Easy. I told him that I was buying Tesla and SpaceX from him, and in exchange, he gets the first Tesla droid with the new built-in exoskeletons and also gets to design 'Mars mode' for that eventuality."

"Mars mode?" Lucas says with a raised eyebrow.

"Yeah, seems like an easy enough ask. If he wants to take his chances on a dead planet, who am I to not enable his fantasy and get what I want, which is securing a bright future for humanity?"

"Well done, Steve...well done. I have to say, I'm very impressed. Your deal-making skills are absolutely mint."

"Thanks, Lucas. Now, we can rest easy knowing we just averted the robot apocalypse." They both stared at each other before bursting out in hearty laughter.

"Yes, we did," Lucas said. "And now, we can set our sights on maxing out the TriBox-alon....."

It was the fall of 2028, and Steve knew that later that night, Lucas was planning to take Coco to his St. Mark's homecoming football game.

"Ha! Wooahhh!" Steve laughed, winked thinking about Lucas' wish, and pointed to the sky using the ASL (American Sign Language) hand sign for 'I love you' and laughed, "You better ask Coco about that. Sometimes, you just have to wait around to catch up with yourself!"

SOMETIMES

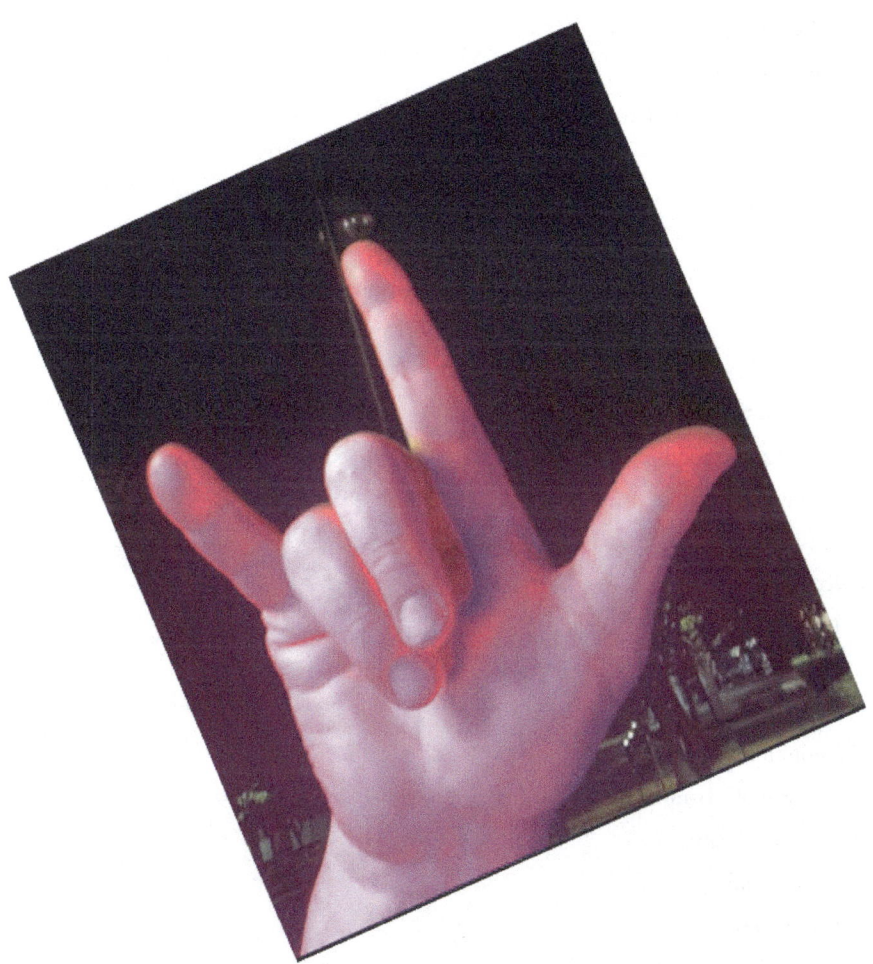

"Sometimes, you just have to wait around to catch up with yourself." Lucas

GUIDING LIGHT MANTRA CHAPTER 11:

    When I wish to be a star
I'm just like those who are
The time will come
When I'll see
Why I've chosen this destiny
Allowing my heart to drive my dream
Sparks a momentum that will seem
To grow and reflect
And bounce around as I inspect

The MAXPOZ™ track
I'll Hop on!
I'll Hop on!
I'll Hop on the MAXPOZ™ track!
    I'll Do some good
Like I knew I would
Ride the train
Direct my brain
    On the MAXPOZ™ Track
On the MAXPOZ™ Track

I'll soon understand
The power of a band that jumps on a team
to drive my dream
to burst ahead and to lead
everyone to see
    the obvious fact of
MAXPOZ™ Impact

COMMENCEMENT

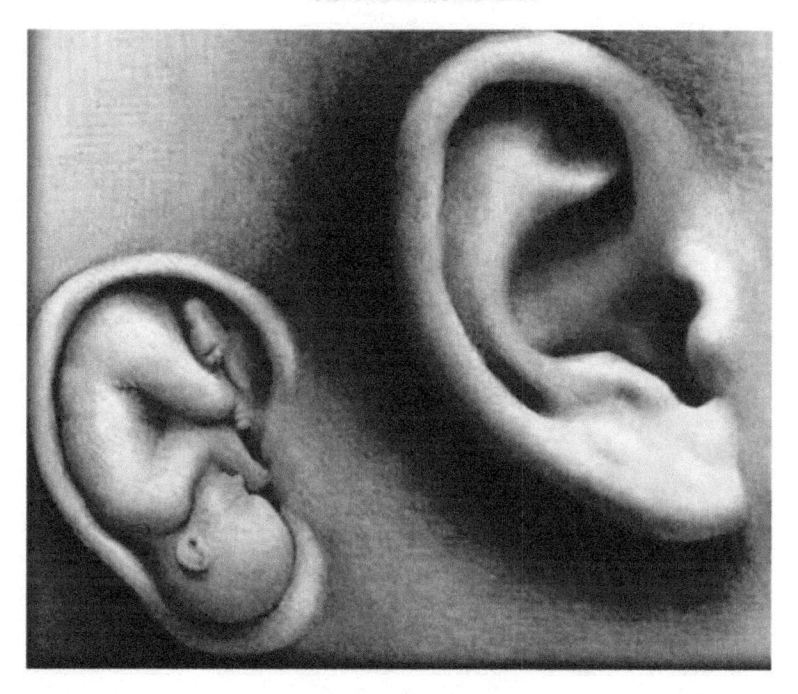

"hEAR" your inner child.

I do believe that you will catch up with your self
and your dreams will come true.

Sincerely,

Elvis Swifty

CODE OF BOUNTY FOUNDATIONAL CREEDS

"The two most important days in your life are the day that you were born and the day you find out why."

—Mark Twain

"The meaning of life is to find your gift. The purpose of life is to give it away."

—Pablo Picasso

"Don't forsake your dreams, and they won't forsake you!"

— Stephen Tobolowsky

CODE OF BOUNTY GUIDING LIGHT MANTRAS

CHAPTER 1:

I will follow my curiosity to unlock the value of the forces of evolution, innovation and creativity in my life.

CHAPTER 2:

I will accept the knowledge that I have a special, unique and irreplaceable gift for humanity.

CHAPTER 3: I love myself with empathy and the knowledge that when I choose to go with the flow, I am doing my very best. Otherwise, I am confident that my intuition will lead me to proactively take decisive action and make meaningful commitments when the time is right.

CHAPTER 4:

The reason that there is no magic bean is because I am the magic.

CHAPTER 5:

Unleashing my inner light will bring the bounty of the world to my door.

CHAPTER 6:

I have the Midas touch. There exists no force that can thwart the life force fueled by the focus of my consciousness.

CHAPTER 7:

Once I commit to stand for my cause, whatever that cause may be, my self-confidence will be forever fortified, and the universe will amplify my message.

CHAPTER 8:

Becoming a champion of my special cause magnifies the focus of my consciousness to effectuate the delivery of my unique gift to the universe.

CHAPTER 9:

The act of standing to deliver results to compete with others enables me to accept wisdom while exercising my mind, spirit and body.

CHAPTER 10:

Connecting in emotionally committed relationships enables me to access the best that humanity has to offer.

CHAPTER 11 GUIDING LIGHT IS ON THE NEXT PAGE —>

CHAPTER 11:

When I wish to be a star
I'm just like those who are
The time will come
When I'll see
Why I've chosen this destiny
Allowing my heart to drive my dream
Sparks a momentum that will seem
To grow and reflect and bounce around
as I inspect
The MAXPOZ™ track
I'll Hop on!
I'll Hop on!
I'll Hop on the MAXPOZ™ track!
I'll Do some good
Like I knew I would
Ride the train
Direct my brain
On the MAXPOZ™ Track
On the MAXPOZ™ Track
I'll soon understand
the power of a band
that jumps on a team
to drive my dream
to burst ahead and
to lead everyone
to see the obvious fact
of MAXPOZ™ Impact
MAXPOZ™
MAXPOZ™ IMPACT!

Chapter Fifteen

PHOTO AND IMAGE CREDITS

Photo / Illustration Credits:

Paul McCartney photo, Photographer/Artist: Robert Whitaker by via Getty Images

Steve Jobs photo, Photographer/Artist: Andy Freeberg by via Getty Images

"The Listener" by Raoof Haghighi.

Mona Lisa by, the painting by Leonardo Da Vinci

Salvator Mundi, the painting by Leonardo Da Vinci

Soulmate, the painting by Stephen Gamson

Elvis Presley photo, Photographer / Artist Sunset Boulevard

Breakfast At Tiffany's photo, Photographer / Artist Donaldson Collection

BeTells Creative Reality TVAgency is United States Trade and Patent Office registered Trademark Reg. No.7,285,131

TriBoxalon is United States Trade and Patent Office registered Trademark Reg. No. 7,277,785

thrivXR is United States Trade and Patent Office registered Trademark Reg. No. 7,278,934

All other non-listed photo credits were produced by and belong to the copyright holder or are in the public domain.

Made in the USA
Monee, IL
01 February 2025